PREPARE

WORKBOOK WITH DIGITAL PACK

A2

LEVEL 3

Frances Treloar   **Second Edition**

Cambridge University Press
www.cambridge.org/elt

Cambridge Assessment English
www.cambridgeenglish.org

Information on this title: www.cambridge.org/9781009030502

© Cambridge University Press & Assessment 2015, 2019, 2021

First published 2015
Second Edition 2019
Second Edition update 2021

20 19 18 17 16 15 14 13 12

Printed in Malaysia by Vivar Printing

A catalogue record for this publication is available from the British Library

ISBN 978-1-00-903050-2 Workbook with Digital Pack
ISBN 978-1-00-902978-0 Student's Book with eBook
ISBN 978-1-00-903064-9 Teacher's Book with Digital Pack

CONTENTS

1 IT'S A CHALLENGE!

VOCABULARY   Adjectives of personality

1 Put the letters in the correct order to make adjectives. The first letter is given.

0	n y u n f	*funny*
1	l o p e i t	p
2	p f l h u e	h
3	r f i n e y l d	f
4	l o u p r a p	p
5	t a v c e i	a
6	n i d k	k
7	z a y l	l
8	u e t i q	q
9	r e v i a c t e	c

2 Complete the sentences with words in Exercise 1.

0 People always laugh at his stories. He's
    funny .

1 On Saturdays, he gets up late and watches TV or funny videos online all day. He's
    .

2 She smiles all the time and talks to everyone. She's   .

3 He always says 'please' and 'thank you' and listens to his teachers. He's   .

4 He cleans his mum's car and always offers to wash the dishes. He's   .

5 Everyone likes her and wants to be her friend. She's   .

6 They go walking or cycling most weekends. They're   .

7 She makes her own clothes and she loves drawing. She's   .

8 He's never angry and always says nice things to people. He's   .

9 She doesn't talk a lot and likes reading and painting. She's   .

GRAMMAR   Present simple and present continuous

1 Add the words and phrases in the box to the table. Do we usually use them with the present simple or present continuous?

> at the moment   every Monday   now   often
> this week   today   twice a week   ~~usually~~

Present simple	Present continuous
usually	

2 Complete the sentences with the present simple or present continuous form of the verbs in brackets.

0 Jake usually   *reads*   stories about detectives. He *'s reading* one about a football player now. (read)

1 My sister   tennis at school every Monday. She   in the park today. (play)

2 Mum often   to music on the radio. But at the moment she   to it on her phone. (listen)

3 My brother usually   his homework in his room. He   it in the library today. (do)

4 My sister   violin lessons twice a week. This week she   a piano lesson, too. (have)

3 Choose the correct verb form to complete the sentences.

1 What *do you usually do / are you usually doing* at the weekends?
2 My mum *teaches / is teaching* me how to make bread at the moment.
3 We *don't go / aren't going* to the park after school on Wednesdays.
4 *Do you have / Are you having* your dinner now?
5 My parents *don't play / aren't playing* golf on Saturdays.

4 Make sentences with the present simple or present continuous.

0 I / do / my homework / at the moment
I'm doing my homework at the moment.
1 They / play / football in the park / now

2 My brother / go / to the cinema / on Friday evenings

3 He / visit / his cousins / on Sunday afternoons

4 My parents / shop / in the supermarket / at the moment

5 We / meet / in the café / every Saturday

6 She / usually / see / her friends / at the weekend

5 Correct the mistakes in the sentences.

0 She is going to work every day, but at the weekend she is free.
She goes to work every day, but at the weekend she is free.
1 Every day in the morning we are eating soup.

2 She study medicine at Odessa University.

3 Anna goes to college every day. She learning English this term.

4 I write this email because I want to tell you about my last trip.

5 My brother plays a board game at the moment because he's bored of computers.

---

1 Read the email. Then complete the personal details below.

Hi! I'm Adam Price, and I'm going to be a student at your school next year. Your teacher, Mr Harrison, gave me your email address because I wanted to say hello before I come. I'm 15 years old, the same as you. Of course, I can speak English because I'm from Australia, but I also speak some Turkish because my mum's from Adana in Turkey. You can email me at **adampr45@kmail.com** and call me on 07662012976. That's my mobile number. I don't have another phone at home.

FIRST NAME: 1) _____

SURNAME: 2) _____

AGE: 3) _____

FIRST LANGUAGE: 4) _____

HOME TELEPHONE: 5) _____

MOBILE: 6) _____

HOME EMAIL ADDRESS: 7) _____

2 Complete the conversation with the shop assistant's questions.

Shop assistant: We don't have the book you want in the shop, but we can send it to you.
Andrew: Great.
Shop assistant: So I'll take some details. First,
¹ _____ ?
Andrew: It's Smith.
Shop assistant: OK. And ² _____ , please?
Andrew: Andrew.
Shop assistant: Thank you. Where do you live?
³ _____ ?
Andrew: It's 34 Charter Street, Witley.
Shop assistant: ⁴ _____ ?
Andrew: It's 07865132467. I don't have a home number.
Shop assistant: OK. ⁵ _____ ?
Andrew: It's andrews567@nextu.com.
Shop assistant: Great. So I'll order the book for you and it'll arrive in seven to ten days.
Andrew: Thank you.

1 Read the blog and choose A or B.

1 The first paragraph gives us
   A a description of Margarita's family.
   B information about the homes of Margarita and her sister.
2 The second paragraph tells us
   A some good things about Sofia.
   B what Sofia is learning to do.
3 The third paragraph is about
   A the activities Sofia is best at.
   B the variety of activities in Sofia's life.
4 Margarita thinks her sister is
   A OK.
   B amazing.

2 Read the blog again and answer the questions.

Margarita's sister
1 What is her first name?

2 What is her surname?

3 How old is she?

4 What is her address?

5 What is her first language?

6 What does she learn about in books?

7 What sport does she do well?

8 What instrument would she like to learn?

DAILY STORIES

by Margarita Marcos

Today I'm writing this blog about my oldest sister, Sofia. She's six years older than me. It's her birthday today and she's 21. She doesn't live in the same house as my parents and me, but her flat is in the same street. We live at number 22 Spring Street, and she lives in one of six flats at number 28.

Sofia is the first person I go to when I have a problem, and she always tries to help. She also helps me with my English homework. We all speak Spanish at home, but Sofia speaks English really well too as a second language. She knows some English from school, but she also listens to English music and watches English films. Another thing she is great at is dancing. She's teaching me the tango this week. Tango is really difficult, but I love the music and the dance.

My sister's interested in everything. She loves learning about science on the internet, and she often reads books about history in her free time. She also does three sports: football, swimming and running. She enjoys them all and is good at swimming. She likes camping, and she's learning to play the piano at the moment, too. She can't play very well yet, but she practises every day. She's also planning to learn the violin. She's a very active person! I really don't know how she has time to do so many things!

LISTENING

🔊 **01**

1 Listen to a teacher talking to his class about a camping trip. Tick (✓) the correct sentences.

In his talk, the teacher
A tells students things they must not do on the trip. ☐
B gives information about activities at the campsite. ☐
C gives information about how they will travel. ☐
D tells students what they must do before the trip. ☐

🔊 **01**

2 Listen again and complete the sentences with a number or a word.

1 The teacher is telling Class _____ about this year's camping trip.
2 Their trip is to _____.
3 They are on the trip for _____ nights.
4 The trip costs £_____.
5 _____ students from the school can go on the trip.
6 At the campsite, you can play _____ in the sports hall.
7 Students can win _____ for cooking and art.
8 Students must give their forms to the teacher on _____ next week.

WRITING   Write an introductory email

1 Read the email. Then match the questions to the answers.

Hi! I'm Aleksey Pavlov, and I'm going to be a student at your school in June. My teacher will send this message to your teacher. I'd like to get to know somebody before I come, so can you email me when you get this? You can email me at **ap8223@rumail.com** and call me on 07662012976. That's my mobile number. I'm fifteen years old and I live on Ligovsky Street in St Petersburg. I live with my mum and my brother. He's eighteen. In my free time I play ice hockey and go to ice hockey matches. I really love ice hockey! I also like cooking. Russian food is fantastic.

I hope to hear from you soon.

Best wishes,

Aleksey

0 First name:	c	**a** ice hockey, cooking
1 Surname:	☐	**b** 07662012976
2 Age:	☐	**c** Aleksey
3 Address:	☐	**d** Ligovsky Street, St Petersburg
4 Email address:	☐	**e** Pavlov
5 Mobile phone number:	☐	**f** 15
6 Family:	☐	**g** Russian
7 Free-time activities he likes:	☐	**h** ap8223@rumail.com
8 Kind of food he likes:	☐	**i** one brother

2 Next year, you are going to spend a month in the UK at a British school. Complete an email like Aleksey's about you.

Hi! I'm _____, and I'm going to be a student at your school in June. My teacher will send this message to your teacher. I'd like to know somebody before I come, so can you email me when you get this?

_____

_____

_____

_____

_____

2 OUR CHANGING PLANET

1 In which photo(s) can you see each geographical feature? Write *A*, *B*, *A and B* or *X* if you cannot see it.

desert	*X*
forest	
hill	
sea	
mountain	
volcano	
valley	
lake	
river	

2 Complete the sentences with the correct form of words in Exercise 1.

1 An example of a _____ is the Nile in Africa.
2 A _____ is a dangerous place. It is very, very hot inside it.
3 The low area between two _____ or mountains is called a _____.
4 The _____ is a large area of water. It has salt in it.
5 Not many plants can grow in a _____. There's a lot of sun and very little rain there.
6 A _____ has lots of trees, plants, animals and birds.

Verbs we don't usually use in the continuous

1 Complete the table with the verbs in the box.

~~believe~~	belong to	~~go~~	happen
hate	have	hope	know
like	love	mean	need
own	read	think	understand
walk	want	watch	write

Verbs that we use in the present continuous	Verbs that we **don't** **usually** use in the present continuous
go	believe

2 Choose the correct verb form to complete the sentences.

1 I *do / 'm doing* my homework now, so I can't come to the park.
2 These books *belong / are belonging* to Simon.
3 I *like / 'm liking* your hat, Tim. Can I try it on?
4 My dad can't take me to football practice because he *works / 's working* at the moment.
5 My mother *understands / 's understanding* some Italian, but she can't speak it very well.
6 *Do you know / Are you knowing* Rachel's brother? He's very funny.
7 I'*m looking for / look for* my new jacket. I can't find it anywhere.
8 I *don't own / 'm not owning* this guitar. It's my sister's.

3 Correct the mistakes in three of the sentences. Which two are correct?

1 There is a concert on Saturday. I am wanting to go.

_____

2 My parents are making dinner at the moment.

_____

3 I think you are liking reading.

_____

4 I don't understand this exercise.

_____

5 We're wanting to tell you what we think of Rio de Janeiro.

_____

Animals

1 Use the definitions and pictures below to complete the crossword.

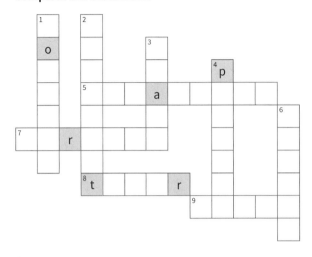

Across

5 This large, heavy animal lives in a very cold part of the world.
7 This animal has a very long neck.
8 This animal lives in jungles, forests or in the mountains. It is a kind of large cat.
9 This animal doesn't have any legs.

Down

1 Picture B
2 Picture C
3 This sea animal is one of the largest animals in the world.
4 Picture A
6 Picture D

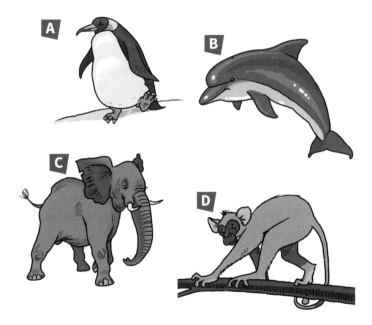

2 What animal do the letters in the grey boxes spell?

_____

OUR CHANGING PLANET 9

READING

1 Read the email from Violetta to her cousin. Choose the correct answers.

1 Violetta is *younger / older* than her brother.
2 Violetta wants to help *people / animals*.
3 Violetta is going to change things in her life because of *the book / her brother*.
4 Violetta knows *nothing / some things* about what Lucia likes.

2 Read the email from Violetta again. There are four sentences missing. Choose the correct place in the email for sentences A–E. There is one extra sentence that you don't need.

A I love animals and I want to know more about how I can help them.
B I'd like to read one of her stories.
C He's at university, studying animal sciences.
D I wrote one last week and he loved it.
E For example, I can stop buying plastic bottles of water, and I can stop using plastic shopping bags.

Hi Lucia,

Thanks for your email. It was good to hear how you are and what you're doing. I love reading too, but I don't know your favourite writer's books. ¹ ....

At the moment, I'm reading a book called *Fast Changing World*. It's not mine; it belongs to my brother. ² .... I don't understand everything in the book; it's for older students, but it's very interesting. It's about what's happening to our planet and how we're losing lots of wild animals and plants because we don't look after our forests, lakes, rivers and seas.

I'm learning so much. The book's giving me some ideas about how I can help stop some of the bad changes happening. ³ .... When these things get into the sea, they're a big problem for fish and sea animals. I talk to my school friends about this, and they want to help too. So one afternoon next week, we're going to spend an afternoon cleaning the beach near my house.

I'd like to study the same subject as my brother, animal sciences, when I go to university. ⁴ .... What do you think, Lucia? I know you're interested in them, but would you like to study animal sciences at university?

Write soon.

Love,

Violetta

LISTENING

PREPARE FOR THE EXAM

Listening Part 5

1 For each question, choose the correct answer.

 You will hear Martha talking to a friend about a trip to the zoo. Which animal was each person most interested in?

People		What they liked best	
0 brother	*E*	**A** bears	**E** monkeys
1 sister	☐	**B** dolphins	**F** penguins
2 dad	☐	**C** elephants	**G** snakes
3 mum	☐	**D** giraffes	**H** wild dogs
4 grandad	☐		
5 grandma	☐		

EXAM TIPS

• Always read the instructions, the questions (1–5) and all the answer options (A–H) before you listen.
• You can only use an answer A–H once. Remember you can't use the example!

1 Read the text and answer the questions.

BLACK BEARS

Black bears live in the forests and mountains of Canada, the USA and Mexico. They usually eat grass and insects, but they eat other things too, including fish, small animals and the food people leave at campsites.

Adults are very big and they weigh between 90 kg and 270 kg. They are tall too: when males stand up on two legs, they are about 180 centimetres tall.

In winter, females have two or three babies, called cubs. They stay with their mother for about two years. Scientists think there are around 600,000 of these animals in the wild in North America, but there may be many more.

0 Which countries do they live in?
Canada, the USA and Mexico

1 What do they eat most of the time?

2 How heavy are they?

3 How many babies do females have?

4 What are their babies called?

5 How long do the babies stay with their mother?

6 How many black bears are there in North America?

2 Read the notes about African elephants. Then write the information in the correct place in the paragraph plan below.

African elephants

leaves, grass, fruit / now 470,000–690,000 wild elephants / forests and grasslands in 37 countries in Africa (Tanzania, Kenya, South Africa, etc.) / live in wild until around 70 / females have one baby ('calf') every two-four years, heavy – about 91 kg when they're born / adults very big – 2,268 kg–6,350 kg

Paragraph 1: where they live / food
forests and grasslands in 37 countries in Africa, ...

Paragraph 2: size / what they weigh / age they live until

Paragraph 3: babies / how many wild African elephants today

3 Use the paragraph plan to write a text about African elephants. When you write about numbers, don't forget to use *between, about / around* and *including*.

3 ON HOLIDAY

Holidays: Ways of travelling

1 Complete the transport words with the missing vowels.

1 p l _ n _
2 b _ k _
3 b _ _ t
4 c _ _ c h

5 h _ l _ c _ pt _ r
6 _ n f _ _ t
7 m _ t _ r b _ k _
8 s c _ _ t _ r

9 s h _ p
10 t r _ m
11 _ n d _ r g r _ _ n d

2 Complete the table with the words in Exercise 1.

What kind of transport travels ...

on the sea?

on a road or path?

on a railway line or track?

in the sky?

plane

3 Match the sentence halves.

1 I need exercise so I go to school ....
2 My dad drives me to school, but we don't have a car. I go to school ....
3 I sail from my home to school across a river. I go to school ....
4 I live very near one of the stations so I go to school ....
5 There are too many cars on the roads, and I often dream of flying to school ....

a by underground.
b by helicopter!
c by motorbike.
d by bike or on foot.
e by boat.

Past simple

1 Complete the sentences with the past simple form of the verbs in brackets.

1 The train to London _____ (be) really fast.
2 Martin's family _____ (go) to Paris by coach because it was the cheapest way.
3 Jane was only 15 but she _____ (know) more than most adults about computers.
4 How _____ you _____ (get) to Moscow?
5 _____ (be) Tom in Ankara or in Istanbul last week?
6 We _____ (not have) a good time on our holiday because we were all ill.
7 There _____ (not be) any trams yesterday because it snowed.

2 Complete the article with the past simple form of the verbs in the box.

arrive   be   do   not stop   spend
start   travel   ~~visit~~   wait

Graham's Big
Adventure

Between 2009 and 2012, Graham Hughes
0 _visited_ all the countries in the world. At that time, there **1** _____ 201 countries. There are now only 195. Graham **2** _____ this without taking a flight. He **3** _____ by boat, bus and train, by taxi and on foot, and he **4** _____ $100 a week on his journey. He **5** _____ his amazing journey on New Year's Day 2009. It was sometimes very difficult. He often **6** _____ for weeks for a boat. But Graham **7** _____, and on Monday 26th November 2012, the 1,426th day of his journey, he **8** _____ in the last country: South Sudan. Graham is the only person to see every country in the world without taking a flight.

3 Correct the mistakes in the sentences.

1 I went to Mar del Plata. I have a lovely day.

_____

2 Last night I forgot my history book in your house.

_____

3 I went shopping yesterday. I brought a very nice skirt and a sweater.

_____

4 I liked the weather last week because it is hot.

_____

4 Which past simple questions need the word *did*?

0 Who _____ – _____ wanted to climb the old tower?
1 Who _____ you see on the plane?
2 Who _____ you go on holiday with?
3 Who _____ flew the plane?
4 Who _____ you meet at the hotel?
5 Who _____ found the bags?
6 Who _____ spoke to the passengers?

VOCABULARY   Holiday vocabulary

1 Put the letters in the correct order to make holiday words. The first letter is given.

1 p m a   m_____
2 s t e g u   g_____
3 t r o i s v i   v_____
4 s c u a i s t e s_____
5 g e u l g a g   l_____
6 p r t c i e i o s e t n   r_____
7 s u t r o i t   t_____
8 u d o g i k e b o   g_____

2 Complete the text with words in Exercise 1.

(H) Highland Hotel

Dear **1** _____,

Welcome to your room at the Highland Hotel! We hope you enjoy staying here.

Everything you need is here at the hotel: two excellent restaurants, two pools and an exercise room.

You will find the rooms are large, with extra space for all your **2** _____ in the cupboard next to the bathroom.

Please also remember that **3** _____s to the museum and the theatre get a 25% discount if they are staying with us. We can give you a **4** _____ of the town so you can easily find these places.

You will also find a small **5** _____ with information about other local tourist attractions in your room.

Please phone the **6** _____ if there is anything else you need. He or she will be happy to help.

From

The Highland Hotel staff team

1 Read the article quickly. What is unusual about this bookshop?

Visiting the *Libreria Acqua Alta* bookshop in Venice

Three young visitors tell us why they liked this unusual place

Elena

The bookshop belongs to Luigi Frizzo. His ideas for the shop are great. During the winter, the sea enters many of the buildings in Venice. But Luigi's books don't get wet because he keeps them in boats and baths instead of bookcases! And not all the books are for people to buy. Old textbooks and dictionaries are now pieces of furniture and art. There are also books on top of each other to make some stairs. I loved climbing up them to the roof and looking out over the city.

Rosie

Last May, I spent a week in Venice with my parents and walked around the city every day. One day, we saw the *Libreria Acqua Alta*, or 'High Water Bookshop' in English. Outside, it looked like other bookshops. We went in because I wanted a map. We then saw it was very different. It wasn't tidy, but was full of wonderful things: thousands of books and about ten friendly cats! This bookshop was my favourite place in Venice.

Christina

I visited *Libreria Acqua Alta* one morning in June and I loved it. Many visitors in the shop felt the same as me. I spoke to a lot, and they were not only tourists. Local families enjoy visiting the shop too because it is so different, and you can find every kind of book there. Luigi Frizzo owns the shop, and he was there that morning. He took me to see the building's fire exit. It was very funny – the door just opens onto the water!

PREPARE FOR THE EXAM

Reading Part 2

2 For each question, choose the correct answer. Write *E* for Elena, *R* for Rosie or *C* for Christina.

1 Which person met Luigi Frizzo?
2 Which person explains why she entered the shop?
3 Which person describes how books stay dry in the bookshop?
4 Which person says what kind of people go to the shop?
5 Which person explains what the name of the bookshop means?
6 Which person saw some books that weren't for sale?
7 Which person describes how books are part of the building?

EXAM TIPS

- Look to see if the writer says the same things in a different way.
- The questions do not follow the order of information in the text.

LISTENING

1 Listen to the conversation between Ross and an assistant in the tourist information office. Match the people to the things they like.

1 Ross's mum likes   **a** football
2 Ross's sister likes   **b** music
3 Ross likes   **c** art
4 Ross's dad likes   **d** old buildings

2 Listen again and choose the correct answers.

0 In Liverpool, there _are two cathedrals_ / _is one cathedral_.
1 Ross likes the idea of the _long / short_ boat trip.
2 You can visit Liverpool Football Club from _10.00 / 10.30_ in the morning.
3 The woman says The Beatles were _fantastic / famous_.
4 Tate Liverpool has _modern art / art from every century_.
5 The assistant gives Ross information about _transport / theatres_.

WRITING   Description of a tourist attraction

1 Read the information about the Basilica Cistern. Then match the parts of the text A–E to the headings below.

1 Details about times and prices
2 Where to go to learn more
3 What this place is
4 Where it is
5 Why you should go there

2 Write about an interesting tourist attraction that you know or would like to visit. Include the same information as the text in Exercise 1.

Hotels   📍 Places to visit   Restaurants   Things to do

If you go to Istanbul, one place you must visit is the Basilica Cistern. **(A)** It is a large area (9,800 m²) under the ground for keeping water. It is around 1,500 years old. **(B)** It is a great place to visit because it is so different to other tourist attractions. It also shows that there were some very good engineers and builders at that time. **(C)** It is open every day from 9.00 in the morning until 5.30 in the evening. Entrance costs 20 Turkish lira. **(D)** It is on Yerebatan Street in the centre of Istanbul. **(E)** You can get further information in English or Turkish on its website.

4 MY PLACE

VOCABULARY Homes

1 Look at the photo. Are the sentences right (✓) or wrong (✗)?

0 This house has a **balcony** above the **garage**. ✓
1 We can see a **sink** inside the garage.
2 The **entrance** to the garden has a **gate**.
3 The garage is on the **ground floor**.
4 The **first floor** of the house has some large windows.
5 There are three black **sofas** on the balcony.
6 There is a **cooker** in the garden.
7 The **ceiling** of the balcony is white.
8 We can see a **lamp** inside the house.
9 There isn't a **cupboard** on the balcony.

2 Complete the answers to the questions with some of the words in bold in Exercise 1.

1 Where do you wash the dishes? in the kitchen ....
2 Where do you keep a car? in a ....
3 What do you open to get into and out of a field or a garden? a ....
4 In a first-floor apartment, where can you go outside? on the ....
5 When you are inside a room, what do you see when you look up? the ....
6 Which floor is below the first floor in a building? the ....
7 In a kitchen, where can you keep plates and cups? in a ....

GRAMMAR Past continuous and past simple

1 Match the sentence halves.

1 I was making a sandwich ....
2 I was sending a text message ....
3 I was playing tennis with my sister ....
4 I was playing an online video game on my laptop ....
5 I was closing the garage door ....

a when my phone stopped working.
b when I remembered the dog was still inside!
c when I cut my finger on the bread knife.
d when I broke my racket.
e when the wi-fi stopped working.

2 Complete the sentences with the correct form of the verbs in brackets.

0 I _was reading_ (read) a book about NASA when Kelly _texted_ (text) me.
1 Marta .... (swim) in the sea when it .... (start) raining heavily.
2 Charlie .... (phone) while you .... (play) football.
3 Dina .... (walk) home from the sports club when she .... (see) her French teacher, Mr Roland.
4 Jim's mum .... (buy) his birthday present while he was .... (play) tennis at the club.
5 Sarah .... (watch) a film in the cinema when someone .... (take) her bag.
6 Bruna and I .... (fly) to London when a storm .... (begin).
7 It was very busy in our house at seven o'clock this morning. While I .... (make) breakfast, my mum .... (talk) on the phone, my dad .... (clean) the floor and my sisters .... (play) with the dog.
8 Katie .... (do) her homework when her best friend .... (arrive) to see her.

3 Correct the three <u>underlined</u> sentences in the email.

```
●●● ◁▷                              🔍 🏠
```

Hi Henry,

How are you? Thanks for your email.

I watched a great football match yesterday – AC Milan against Inter Milan. Inter won 3–0. [1] <u>I was watching it with my family.</u> We really enjoyed it.

After the match, we had a party for my sister. It was her 15th birthday. At the party there were a lot of people. [2] <u>We are dancing, eating and drinking.</u> We had a great time.

You asked me about my holiday in Spain. Well, I enjoyed it very much. We did lots of things. We swam in the sea. We went for long walks. We played basketball. [3] <u>We were lying on the beach every day.</u> We ate meals in nice restaurants. I made friends with a boy and girl from Ireland.

Love,

Petra

1 ....

2 ....

3 ....

1 Find ten more adjectives.

p	u	n	u	s	u	a	l	q	t	c
r	d	l	q	e	p	c	o	l	d	o
t	o	l	u	j	n	n	d	g	a	o
i	e	i	b	r	i	g	h	t	r	l
n	d	g	w	e	z	c	s	j	k	c
y	f	h	a	t	t	e	t	e	n	o
a	t	t	r	a	c	t	i	v	e	s
l	a	d	m	o	v	b	o	k	m	y
p	e	a	c	e	f	u	l	j	x	t

2 What adjective do the letters in the grey boxes spell?

....

3 Choose the correct words to complete the sentences.

1 The weather in my country is really hot in the summer, so it is difficult to keep our house *warm* / *cool*.

2 You can't hear anything in my bedroom, only the birds in the garden – it's very *unusual* / *peaceful*.

3 It is *cosy* / *unusual* for a 15-year-old to have their own flat.

4 It's always very *light* / *dark* in our house because all the rooms have really big windows.

5 Tourists often take photos of my uncle and aunt's house because it is so big and *cosy* / *attractive*.

6 I always sit on our big sofa to watch TV because it is the most *comfortable* / *unusual* place to sit in our flat.

7 My sister is painting her apartment yellow and pink. She loves *bright* / *dark* colours.

4 Write a description of the home of someone you know. Use adjectives in Exercise 1.

....

....

....

....

....

1 Read the descriptions of the houses 1–3 and match them to the photos A–C.

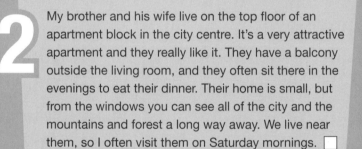

1 My cousin lives in this home with her mother, father and grandma. It's in a quiet part of a large city. The rooms inside it are not big, and it is not the best place for very tall people. But my cousin likes living there because she can travel and be at home at the same time! I love visiting them. I sleep on a sofa in the sitting room because the bedrooms are so small. ☐

2 My brother and his wife live on the top floor of an apartment block in the city centre. It's a very attractive apartment and they really like it. They have a balcony outside the living room, and they often sit there in the evenings to eat their dinner. Their home is small, but from the windows you can see all of the city and the mountains and forest a long way away. We live near them, so I often visit them on Saturday mornings. ☐

3 My grandfather built this house with his father 50 years ago. It is the first house my grandparents lived in after they got married in 1975, and they still live there. My mum lived there when she was a girl. It's a big, quiet house, and it's cosy and warm in the winter when it's cold outside. The garden is really big and is full of trees. My grandparents love living in the house and I enjoy staying there. I spend two weeks there every summer. ☐

2 Which home does each sentence refer to? Write *1*, *2* or *3*. Sometimes more than one answer is possible.

0 There is a garden here. _____3_____
0 Members of the writer's family live here. __1, 2, 3__
1 You can go from place to place in this home. ....
2 We know the age of this home. ....
3 Two people live in this home. ....
4 This home is on land. ....
5 This home is in a city. ....
6 The writer goes and stays here. ....
7 This home is large. ....
8 You need a lift to get to this home. ....

PREPARE FOR THE EXAM

Listening Part 1

1 For each question, choose the correct picture.

1 What was Richard doing when his mum got home?

A 　B 　C

2 What do Charlie and his family use their garage for?

A 　B 　C

3 What did Rosie's dad buy yesterday?

A 　B 　C

4 Who is on the balcony?

A 　B 　C

5 What did Emma paint on her ceiling?

A 　B 　C

 EXAM TIPS

- Listen carefully to the recording both times it is played.
- Look at the pictures and think about the question before you listen.

WRITING　A story

PREPARE FOR THE EXAM

Writing Part 7

1 Look at the three pictures. Write the story shown in the pictures. Write **35 words** or more.

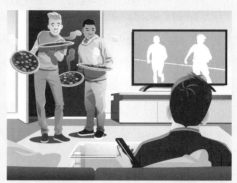

 EXAM TIPS

- You can write the story about the picture in the present or the past.
- You can give the people names.

5 SCHOOL

VOCABULARY | School subjects

1 Match the two halves of the words. Then write the whole words below.

a his   **b** bio   **c** ence   **d** mat
e geo   **f** hs   **g** dra   **h** logy
i sics **j** phy   **k** istry **l** sci
m chem **n** tory **o** ma   **p** graphy

0 *a + n = history*   **4** ....
1 ....   **5** ....
2 ....   **6** ....
3 ....   **7** ....

2 Choose the correct answers.

1 I want to work with numbers, so I need to study ....
   A biology   **B** maths   **C** science
2 I want to travel to other countries, so I need to study ....
   A drama   **B** foreign languages   **C** PE
3 I want to write computer programmes, so I need to study ....
   A chemistry   **B** geography   **C** ICT
4 I want to be an actor, so I need to study ....
   A maths   **B** history   **C** drama
5 I want to help find new medicines, so I need to study ....
   A design and technology   **B** biology   **C** history

3 Write the correct subject. Do <u>not</u> use *science*.

In which subject do you do these things?

1 play basketball ....
2 learn about rivers, mountains and oceans ....
3 learn about facts from the past ....
4 draw something then make it ....
5 learn about using numbers ....
6 study how plants grow ....
7 learn about space, the moon and the stars ....
8 learn about computers and using the internet ....
9 speak, hear, read and write lots of new words from a different country ....

GRAMMAR | Comparative and superlative adverbs

1 Read the situations. Are sentences 1–8 right (✓) or wrong (✗)?

Ben speaks more quickly than Greg. Ronan speaks the most quickly.
1 Ronan speaks more slowly than Greg. ....
2 Greg speaks the slowest. ....

In the basketball match, Reeta played better than Sarah. Kiera played the best.
3 Reeta played worse than Kiera. ....
4 Reeta played the worst. ....

Nick learns maths more slowly than David. Martin learns maths the most quickly.
5 Martin learns maths more easily than Nick. ....
6 Nick learns maths the most easily. ....

Izzie and Maria did their homework very quickly on the school bus. Paloma did hers more slowly at home.
7 Izzie did her homework more carefully than Maria. ....
8 Paloma did her homework the most carefully. ....

2 Complete the sentences with the comparative or superlative form of the adjectives in brackets.

1 Mrs Black speaks .... than the other teachers. (quiet)
2 Toni plays volleyball .... of all the players on our team. (well)
3 Chris runs .... than Sam. (quick)
4 Nobody did well in the history exam, but I did .... of all. (bad)
5 Jim, Norman and Ian worked together on a group project, but Norman worked .... in the group. (hard)

3 Complete the sentences with *more* or *most*.

1 We can all sing in my family, but my brother can sing the .... beautifully of all of us.
2 Mr Sanchez explains things .... carefully than Mr Wright. I prefer Mr Sanchez!
3 My brother learns languages .... easily than I do. He can speak English, French and Russian.
4 Sara speaks the .... quickly of all the people in the class. I never understand what she says!
5 For me, maths is the .... difficult subject at school. I have to do lots of extra practice to pass the exams.

4 Put the words in the correct order to make sentences.

1 more / Jacob / the meal / quickly / his friends / finished / than

2 carefully / Davina / her name / most / wrote / the

3 works / than / Louis / the other art students / harder

4 the / sleeps / worst in her family / always / Marta

5 Choose the correct words to complete the sentences.

1 I speak German *better* / *well* than my brother.
2 Every day at the college you learn lots of words in English, and this helps you to speak English more *easy* / *easily*.
3 Today is my birthday. Everyone gave me presents. The present I *like the best* / *best like* is the computer my parents gave me.
4 My father drives more *careful* / *carefully* than my uncle.
5 Our Spanish teacher explains things *clearer* / *more clearly* than our French teacher.

VOCABULARY *take*

1 Read the sentences. Match the meanings of *take* to the verbs in the box.

carry	catch	~~do~~	go along
make	study	use	

0 I have to **take** my geography exam again.
  do
1 We're going to **take** a train to Edinburgh in the morning.
2 Don't forget to **take** your key. I won't be at home when you get back.
3 I should **take** some medicine because I've got a bad cold.
4 **Take** the first turning on the left. The cinema is on the right.
5 I always **take** lots of photographs on holiday.
6 Everyone at my school has to **take** maths and science.

2 Look at the photos. What are the people doing? Write sentences using *take*.

0 *She is taking a photo.*
1 ....
2 ....
3 ....
4 ....

Brooklyn Free School

1 Read the blog quickly. Is this school the same as your school or is it different?

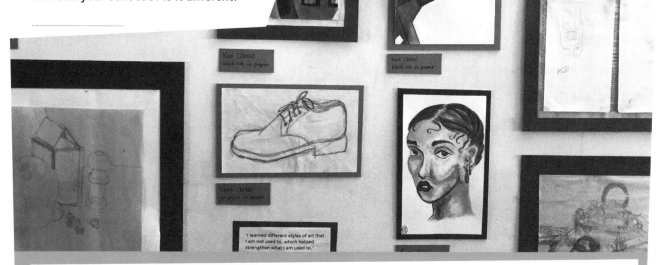

"I learned different styles of art that I am not used to, which helped strengthen what I am used to."

Brooklyn Free School has one part for students aged 11–18 and one for students aged 4–11. Students in both parts choose the subjects they take, never do homework and don't have to take exams or tests. And if they're not enjoying a chemistry lesson, for example, they can walk out, or go to the students' room and read a book. Three younger kids were doing this when I went in there on my visit. Other examples of subjects on the timetable are writing films and building design – a very popular subject.

Some people think this kind of school is a bad idea. They don't think it teaches students the things they'll need when they grow up. They also think the school's only for people who have lots of money. But actually, only 20% of the students pay the whole cost of being at the school.

So what do the students think? One student, Marlon, says in his favourite class he watched a TV show about city life. It taught him a lot. In another, students discussed how people decide about things or vote. They then ate at local restaurants and decided which one they liked the best. Marlon also enjoyed making models of other students in a design class.

But Marlon found it hard when he started at the school. It took more than a year for him to feel comfortable there. He played computer games in the students' room for most of that first year. Now he enjoys classes and says he wouldn't like to go to school anywhere else.

PREPARE FOR THE EXAM

Reading Part 3

2 For each question, choose the correct answer.

1 What does the first paragraph tell us about Brooklyn Free School?
 A Only students aged 11–18 can decide to go to a class or not.
 B Both older and younger students can choose their subjects.
 C The older students have lessons with the younger students.

2 The writer saw some children at the school
 A leaving a chemistry lesson.
 B reading books instead of going to lessons.
 C enjoying a building design lesson.

3 The writer explains why it is not true to say that
 A there are too few students at the school.
 B the school doesn't teach students useful things.
 C only rich students can go to the school.

4 What did Marlon enjoy doing the most?
 A learning about city life
 B going to restaurants
 C making models of people

5 How does Marlon feel about the school?
 A He is happier there now than he was.
 B He likes it because he can play computer games there.
 C He wants to try another type of school.

EXAM TIPS

• Read the text once before you answer the questions.
• After you choose your answer, look at the text to check that the other answers are wrong.

1 Listen to three people talking about school and learning. Write *Mrs Black*, *Lorna* or *Ben*.

1 _____ is describing a school.
2 _____ is describing a way of learning.
3 _____ is explaining what is going to happen.

2 Listen again and write one word or number for each answer.

A
1 What subject will Mrs Black teach Class 8A?

_____

2 What subject will Mr Hill teach Class 8A?

_____

B
3 Where does Lorna live?
on a _____
4 Who is homeschooled with Lorna?
her _____
5 What subject does their mum teach the best?

_____

C
6 Where is the best school for Ben's son?
in _____ Street
7 How many students are there at the school?

_____

8 What can't students wear to the school?

_____

9 How often do students at the school take tests?
every _____

A description of your perfect school

1 Read the text about someone's perfect school. Then match the parts of the text A–G to the questions below.

0 What homework do you have? _____ *E*
1 How long are the holidays? _____
2 What lessons do you have? _____
3 Who are the teachers? _____
4 Where is the school? _____
5 What do you wear to school? _____
6 How many students are there at the school? _____

My PERFECT school

(A) I love animals so my perfect school is in a zoo. **(B)** There are only three students at the school: me and my two best friends, Carla and Monica. They love animals, too. **(C)** Our teachers are the zoo keepers*. They teach us everything they know about their animals. **(D)** We don't have subjects like maths or history at my perfect school. The only subjects we take are geography and biology. We learn about different kinds of animals from different countries, and we learn about animal biology and medicine. **(E)** We have homework, but it's not reading or writing. It is doing things with the animals, like taking baby animals home and giving them food during the night, for example. **(F)** We have a uniform. It is green trousers and shirts, and boots. **(G)** We don't need holidays because we love going to our school.

* zoo keepers are people that work in a zoo and look after the animals

2 Write about your perfect school. Answer the questions in Exercise 1 and add anything else you want to say.

_____
_____
_____
_____
_____
_____
_____
_____
_____
_____

6 FAVOURITE THINGS

VOCABULARY — Materials

1 Are the sentences right (✓) or wrong (✗)?

1 Shoes are never made of leather. ....
2 Books are always made of wool. ....
3 Lots of tables and chairs are made of wood. ....
4 Coats are usually made of paper. ....
5 Bottles are often made of plastic. ....

2 Complete the answers to the questions with the words in the box.

cotton	glass	gold	leather
plastic	silver	wood (x2)	wool

1 Which two materials come from animals?
.... and ....
2 Which material do we use to make paper?
....
3 Which two materials are kinds of metal?
.... and ....
4 Which material do we use to make mirrors and windows?
....
5 Which material do we use to make phone cases?
....
6 Which two materials come from plants?
.... and ....

3 Write two sentences about what the things in the photos are made of.

0 The lamp: metal or plastic?
The lamp isn't made of plastic. It's a metal lamp.
1 The box: wool or wood?
....
2 The bottles: glass or silver?
....
3 The bag: cotton or leather?
....
4 The table: wood or glass?
....

GRAMMAR — Possession

1 Look at the pictures and tick (✓) the correct sentences.

0 Who does the guitar belong to?
  A It's my friend's. ✓
  B It's my friends'. ....

1 Who does the cat belong to?
  A It's my cousins'. ....
  B It's my cousin's. ....

2 Who does the computer belong to?
  A It belongs to friends of his. ....
  B It belongs to a friend of theirs. ....

3 Who does the present belong to?
  A It's their daughters'. ....
  B It's their daughter's. ....

2 Choose the correct word to complete the sentences.

1 Don't touch that. It's *my* / *mine.*
2 That's his suitcase, and those are *their* / *theirs* suitcases.
3 Helen, I've got *yours* / *your* video game.
4 Juan's got two brothers. They're friends of *my* / *mine.*
5 This jumper is his, and that one is *yours* / *your.*
6 These surfboards are *our* / *ours.* That one's mine.
7 Are these shoes *her* / *hers*? Or are they his?

3 Complete the sentences with *s*, *'s* or *s'*.

1 My grandmother _____ cat is 22 years old!
2 My best friend _____ names are Holly and Lorna.
3 Is this laptop your _____?
4 There are lots of toys in the children _____ bedroom.
5 Those bags are our _____ – mine is the blue one and Luke _____ is the red one.

4 Correct the mistakes in the sentences.

👁 1 I watched a volleyball's game last Friday.
_____

2 The colour of mine bedroom is blue.
_____

3 I bought a smartphone. You can take great photos with it's camera.
_____
_____

4 I went to the football match with my father and two friends of us.
_____
_____

5 I bought a pair of jeans because mines are small.
_____

1 Match the words to their meanings.

1	nice to look at	**a**	large
2	not square	**b**	small, little
3	not big	**c**	lovely, pretty
4	not hard	**d**	old
5	big	**e**	round
6	not new	**f**	soft

2 Match the sentence halves.

1 My uncle and aunt live in an
2 These shoes are
3 My pillows feel so
4 Your scarf is
5 My mother gave me this lovely necklace

a soft. I love sleeping on them!
b old house next to the sea.
c so small. I wore them when I was a boy.
d when I was a little girl.
e really pretty. Where did you buy it?

3 Complete the sentences with the words in the box.

colourful	hard	heavy
round	smooth	soft

1 If you are not careful when you carry large, _____ things, you can hurt your back.
2 My grandma always wears _____ clothes. She never wears grey or black.
3 Oranges, balls, rings and the world are all _____.
4 If ice cream doesn't have little pieces of fruit or chocolate in it, it is _____.
5 Old bread is dry and _____.
6 Clothes made from wool are usually _____ and warm.

READING

1 Read the messages and choose the correct answer.

Who is Harry?

A William's dad
B William's friend
C William's brother

Hi Hasan, I can't find my jacket. Did I leave it at your house yesterday afternoon when Harry and I came to see your new scooter? It's a soft green jacket. I wore it to walk to your house, and I put it over that big wooden chair in your hall. I can't remember if I wore it to walk home. I hope you've got it – it cost a lot!

Hi William, I have got your jacket, yes. I just went to look in the hall, and it was on the chair, as you thought. And I also found another jacket on that chair. It's a black, leather one. It's not mine and it's not my brother's. Do you think it's Harry's? I'm not going out this evening. So you can come and get your jacket then if you want to.

Hi Hasan, that's great. I'm so glad it's there. My dad will be too – he bought it for me. I can come to your place at about six. Is that OK? I think that other jacket is Harry's. He was wearing a black leather jacket when we walked to your house. I can get it when I come to get mine – then I'll give it to him tomorrow. I'm going out for the day with his family. I'll call him and tell him his jacket's at yours.

2 Read the messages again and complete the sentences with one word.

0 William can't find his _____jacket_____.
1 William went to Hasan's house to see his new _____.
2 The chair in Hasan's hall is made of _____.
3 The black jacket is a _____ jacket.
4 The black jacket is not Hasan's, it's not William's and it's not Hasan's _____.
5 Hasan says that William can get his jacket in the _____.
6 William thinks his _____ will be happy because his jacket is not lost.
7 William wants to go to Hasan's at _____ o'clock.

LISTENING

✓ **PREPARE FOR THE EXAM**

Listening Part 5

1 For each question, choose the correct answer.

 You will hear Alicia talking to her Aunt Jane about packing things in boxes to take to a new house. Who does each thing belong to?

Things		People
0 tennis racket	F	**A** George
1 phone	☐	**B** Alicia
2 book	☐	**C** Aunt Jane
3 video games	☐	**D** Ben
4 photo	☐	**E** Ryan
5 keys	☐	**F** Alicia's dad
		G Alicia's mum
		H Daniel

 EXAM TIPS

• The questions (1–5) are in the same order as the recording.
• When you have used an answer, ~~cross it out~~.

WRITING — Adjective order

1 Complete the table with the words in the box.

~~big~~	black	~~cotton~~	glass	~~green~~	hard	heavy	large	little	lovely	metal	new
old	pretty	round	silver	small	smooth	~~soft~~	~~square~~	~~ugly~~	wooden	~~young~~	

Opinion	Size	Physical quality	Shape	Age	Colour	Material
ugly	big	soft	square	young	green	cotton

2 Complete each sentence with three different adjectives in Exercise 1 and put them in the correct order.

0 We all love our _lovely, little, black_ dog.

1 We need a _____ sofa in our sitting room. We haven't got any comfortable chairs in there.

2 My sister got a _____ necklace for her birthday. Now it's her favourite thing in the world.

3 I don't understand why my mum bought that _____ lamp. It's horrible!

4 The _____ building at the end of my street is very interesting.

3 Read the article from a school magazine and answer the questions.

1 What is the important object?

2 Where is it from?

3 What adjectives does the writer use to describe it?

4 Why is it important to the writer?

5 What does the writer like about it?

4 Write an email to the school magazine about something important to you. Answer the questions below.

1 What is it?
2 What does it look like?
3 Who and / or where is it from?
4 Why is it important to you?
5 What do you like about it?

To: news@hftschool.org   Reply Forward

WHAT THINGS ARE IMPORTANT TO YOU?

I have a beautiful, old, wooden bowl. It comes from Germany and was made in about 1930. It is important to me because it belonged to my grandmother's German mother. I like it because it feels really strong and smooth, and it's like part of our family!

We would like to know what is important to you. Email us at news@hftschool.org. We will put the best three entries in next month's edition.

7 ADVENTURE HOLIDAYS

Holiday activities

1 Match the two parts of the holiday activities. Only one answer is <u>not</u> a two-word phrase. Which one?

1	horse	**a**	surfing
2	mountain	**b**	skiing
3	water	**c**	biking
4	zip	**d**	boarding
5	paddle	**e**	wiring
6	kite	**f**	riding

2 Complete the sentences with the holiday activities.

camping   diving   hiking   sailing

1 I like .... because I love being on a boat on the sea.
2 I like .... because I love seeing all the different animals under the water.
3 I like .... because I love sleeping and cooking outside.
4 I like .... because I love going from place to place on foot.

3 Match the phrasal verbs to the definitions.

1	get back	**a**	leave your bed
2	get lost	**b**	go into a bus, train, plane or boat
3	get on		
4	get to	**c**	arrive in a place
5	get up	**d**	not know where you are
		e	return from somewhere to a place you were before

4 Complete the conversation with the words in Exercise 3.

Carla: How are you getting ¹ .... Edinburgh?
Marko: By train. We've got to get ² .... at 5.30 tomorrow morning. We're getting ³ .... the train at Parkside station, and it takes an hour to drive there from our flat.
Carla: That's very early, Marko.
Marko: I know. We'll be tired. I hope we don't get ⁴ .... when we're driving to the train station. I don't know the way very well.
Carla: When are you getting ⁵ .... from Edinburgh?
Marko: On Monday evening at about seven o'clock.
Carla: Well, have a great time!

Present continuous for future

1 Complete the sentences with the present continuous form of the verbs in brackets.

1 Laura .... (meet) her cousin for lunch next Monday.
2 Stefan and his dad .... (play) tennis next Friday.
3 I .... (study) Chinese next Thursday.
4 We .... (take) our brother to the zoo next Tuesday.
5 Lucinda .... (have) a birthday party next Saturday.
6 Eliot .... (visit) his grandparents next Sunday.

2 Match the pictures with the sentences in Exercise 1.

3 Correct the mistakes in the sentences.

👁 **1** I'm going to the airport. My mum arrive at 3.30 pm.
....

2 My father takes us to the sports centre at six o'clock. Don't forget to bring your racket!
....

3 Would you like to help me paint my bedroom? We starting on Sunday morning at 10.
....

4 My friend Jacek is from Poland. Next week he come to see us in England.
....

5 Don't forget we meet at 3 pm at my house.
....

4 Write four sentences about things you are doing this year. Use the present continuous and a month or a date.

0 *Gonzalo and I are playing in a table tennis competition on 4th June.*
1 ....
2 ....
3 ....
4 ....

VOCABULARY — Things to take on an adventure holiday

1 Use the definitions to complete the crossword.

[crossword grid with numbers 1, 2, 3, 4, 5, 6, 7, 8, 9, 10, 11, 12, 13]

Across

1 You use this after a shower or bath.
5 You lie down in this at night.
6 You carry all your things in this.
8 You stay in this when you're camping.
9 You look at this for information if you get lost.
11 .... cream
13 You need this if you hurt yourself.

Down

1 It gives light.
2 You put your toothbrush, toothpaste and soap in this.
3 You wear these for running.
4 You eat this.
7 This tells you which way to go, e.g. north, south, east or west.
10 .... boots
12 You wear this on the top part of your body: waterproof ....

2 Complete the conversation with the correct form of words in Exercise 1.

Mum: So, Nadya. Have you got everything for your hiking trip in your ¹ ....? It looks full and heavy!

Nadya: I think so. I just need to put my ² .... on the top – it will be lovely and warm for nights in the mountains.

Mum: Your new ³ .... are by your bed. Are you wearing them?

Nadya: Yes, and I'm taking just one other pair of shoes – my trainers. I'm also wearing jeans, a sweater and my ⁴ .... over the top so I don't get wet.

Mum: OK. Have you packed a ⁵ .... for drying yourself?

Nadya: Of course I have! And I've got my ⁶ .... with soap and toothpaste in it.

Mum: Great. You'll need to take some ⁷ .... as well.

Nadya: I know. I'll get some fruit and some biscuits.

Mum: Sounds good. Now what's that piece of paper on the bed?

Nadya: Oh no! That's the ⁸ .... showing where we have to walk! I'm so glad you saw that, Mum!

1 Read the email and choose the correct answers.

A Erin asks Katie and Pippa to go with her to the beach for a weekend.
B Erin tells Katie and Pippa about her favourite activities.
C Erin describes a trip on a boat.
D Erin tells Katie and Pippa what things to bring.
E Erin tells Katie and Pippa where to find more information.
F Erin asks Katie and Pippa to choose some activities to do at the weekend.

Hi Katie and Pippa!

I hope you're not busy Saturday 16th and Sunday 17th August. Brett Beach Surfing Club is having a family fun weekend. My mum and dad want to take me and two of my friends. I'd love you both to come. We're taking a tent so we can stay at the beach.

It's perfect for you both. There are loads of different activities happening – waterskiing, horse riding, kite surfing, and swimming and running races. There's a diving trip on Sunday morning, too. You can try all of the activities, and some of them are free. You only pay for the horse riding, waterskiing and diving trip. There are also activities in the evenings. On Saturday, there's an evening trip on a beautiful old wooden boat called *The Blue Adventure*. You go out to sea and have dinner on the boat, 'watching the stars, the sea animals playing and the pretty lights along the coast' (that's what it says on the website!). And later some bands are playing on the beach. It all looks really cool. What do you think?

I really hope you can come. You won't need to bring a lot – our tent's big and we've got all the camping kit. You'll just need to bring your sleeping bag, your swimming costume and a few clothes in your backpack. Mum will bring loads of towels and things like that for us all. Here's the website link so you can see more: **www.bbsc.com/bigfamfun**. Let me know what you think soon!

Lots of love,

Erin

2 Are the sentences right (✓) or wrong (✗)?

1 Erin is going to the family fun weekend with her parents.
2 Erin is going camping at the beach for a weekend.
3 Erin thinks Katie and Pippa will enjoy the weekend a lot.
4 The horse riding is free.
5 Erin doesn't think *The Blue Adventure* looks very nice.
6 There is music on the beach on Saturday night.
7 Katie and Pippa will need to take a tent.
8 Katie and Pippa will need to take some towels.

✓ PREPARE FOR THE EXAM

Listening Part 2

1 For each question, write the correct answer in the gap.
🔊 Write **one word** or **a number** or **a time**.

07 You will hear a teacher telling students about a trip.

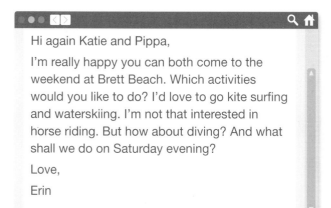

School Trip

Name of the island: _Dolphin_ Island

Time boat leaves: (1) ....

Place for lunch on the island: (2) ....

Age of the castle: (3) .... years old

Activity: (4) ....

Person to call for help: (5) Mrs ....

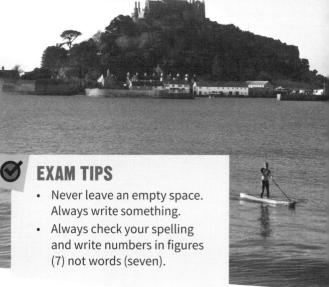

✓ EXAM TIPS

- Never leave an empty space. Always write something.
- Always check your spelling and write numbers in figures (7) not words (seven).

WRITING An email reply to a suggestion

1 Read Erin's email and Pippa's reply. Which part of Pippa's reply …

A makes a suggestion? ....

B disagrees with Erin's suggestions? .... and ....

C agrees with Erin's suggestion? ....

🔍 🏠

Hi again Katie and Pippa,

I'm really happy you can both come to the weekend at Brett Beach. Which activities would you like to do? I'd love to go kite surfing and waterskiing. I'm not that interested in horse riding. But how about diving? And what shall we do on Saturday evening?

Love,

Erin

🔍 🏠

Hi Erin,

I'm really excited about the weekend at Brett Beach! [1] It's a great idea to go kite surfing, [2] but I'm not that interested in waterskiing. [3] I'd also prefer not to go diving. [4] On Saturday evening, why don't we go to listen to the music on the beach? That sounds great.

Love,

Pippa

---

2 Imagine you are Katie and write a reply to Erin. Look back at the poster on page 30 to help you.

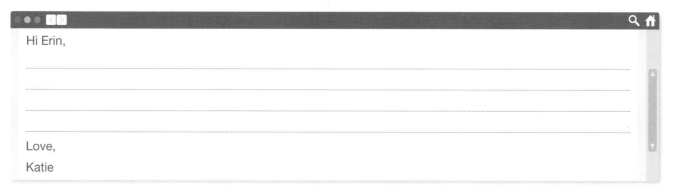

🔍 🏠

Hi Erin,

....

....

....

....

Love,

Katie

8 LIFE IN THE FUTURE

VOCABULARY Furniture and household appliances

1 In which photo can you see each word below? Write *A*, *B*, *A and B* or *X* if you cannot see it.

0	roof	*X*
1	a bin	
2	a washing machine	
3	a fridge	
4	a bookcase	
5	air conditioning	
6	a barbecue	
7	some stairs	
8	a drawer	
9	a light	
10	seats	
11	heating	

2 Complete the sentences with the words in the box.

> air conditioning   bookcase   fridge
> heating   lights   roof   stairs
> washing machine

1 When you need some clean clothes, use a
....

2 When you need to make your house warmer, turn on your ....

3 When your classroom is too hot, turn on the ....

4 When you need to go to the first floor from the ground floor, walk up the
....

5 When your bedroom's too dark, switch on the ....

6 When you want a cold drink, get one from the ....

7 When you want something to read, go and choose something from the
....

8 If rain comes into your house, perhaps there's a problem with the
....

GRAMMAR Future with *will, may* and *might*

1 Put the words in the correct order to make sentences and questions.

1 I / to the cinema / I'll go / don't think / .

2 win / the Champions League / will / Chelsea / ?

3 will / the weather / get better / I think / .

4 Chris / do you think / his history exam / will pass / ?

5 won't win / our team / the championship / .

6 be very different / will life / in the future / ?

2 Complete the sentences with the correct form of *will*. Use the verbs in brackets. Do you agree with the predictions?

0 I think we *'ll live* on Mars. (live)

1 What _____ life _____ like in the future? (be)

2 We _____ much longer than we do today. (not live)

3 We _____ the internet. There will be something new. (not have)

4 I think we _____ things on and off in our houses just by thinking about it. (turn)

5 I don't think we _____ paper money. (use)

3 Read the text and complete the sentences below with *will*, *won't*, *may* or *might*. Sometimes more than one answer is possible.

Gerry is going to the cinema this weekend. Only one of his friends can go with him: Pete. The cinema is closed in the morning and the afternoon. There are two films on at the cinema: *Cloud Thirteen* and *Heat*. Gerry usually walks to the cinema because he can't drive, but Pete can.

What will happen this weekend?

1 Gerry _____ go to the cinema with Pete.
2 Gerry _____ go to the cinema with his friend Jack.
3 Gerry _____ watch *Heat* at the cinema.
4 Gerry _____ go to the cinema in the evening.
5 Gerry _____ get a lift with Pete to the cinema.
6 Gerry _____ drive to the cinema.

4 Read the text in Exercise 3 again. Write two more sentences about what Gerry will, might, may or won't do this weekend.

1 _____
2 _____

5 Correct the mistakes in the sentences.

1 Just come to my house and we have a great time together.
_____

2 Wear old clothes because we probably get paint on them.
_____

3 What time do you come?
_____

4 I am arrive at eleven o'clock.
_____

5 I think that you can only need £5 for the skate park.
_____

VOCABULARY Words with two meanings

1 Complete the table with the words in the box. Some words can go in more than one column. Use a dictionary to help you.

| book | kind | letter |
| picture | ring | watch |

Verbs	Nouns	Adjectives

2 Complete the sentences with the correct form of the words in Exercise 1. Use the same word twice.

1 I'd like to make a cake for you because you're so _____ to me. What _____ of cake do you like?
2 My grandad writes _____ to me. They're difficult to read because he writes with such small _____.
3 I read in my _____ about Milan that Giacomo is one of the best restaurants in the city, so I _____ a table for us.
4 I was _____ TV last night when I saw an advert for a new _____. If you ask it the time, it tells you.
5 We'll _____ you when your silver _____ is ready to collect, Miss Jenson.
6 Did you draw that _____? Can I take a _____ of it with my phone?

READING

1 Read the text quickly and choose the best title.

  A Hotels in the future
  B Future homes and holidays

A new report about the future shows us how our work, home and free time might be in a hundred years' time. In the report, a **(1)** _____ of scientists and designers give their ideas about the future.

They say many buildings will be much higher than the tallest buildings now. We'll also build homes with lots of floors under the ground. But we won't only build on **(2)** _____. There may be homes, and **(3)** _____ whole cities, under the sea, too.

Inside homes, we can already turn on things like the **(4)** _____ with our phones. In the future, we'll do more from our phones. And the walls inside our homes will move so we can change the shape of rooms **(5)** _____. Nobody will paint their homes. Every home will have special **(6)** _____ to give the walls different colours and pictures at different times.

One of the most amazing ideas in the report is that we will take our own homes with us on holiday! People will have special holiday homes, full of all their things, and carry them to their holiday place. We will use large drones (objects that fly without a pilot) to do this. This may mean that people won't use hotels in the future. And when we are bored of that, instead of going away to the beach or another country, we will leave the world and fly to the moon or go to another planet.

✓ PREPARE FOR THE EXAM

Reading Part 4

2 For each question, choose the correct answer.

1 A class	**B** group	**C** kind
2 A place	**B** land	**C** area
3 A still	**B** really	**C** perhaps
4 A heating	**B** roof	**C** drawer
5 A carefully	**B** happily	**C** easily
6 A stairs	**B** lights	**C** seats

✓ EXAM TIPS

- Read the text quickly before you answer the questions.
- After you answer the questions, read the complete text again.

3 Read the text again. Then tick (✓) the correct answers for each question (1 and 2).

1 Which questions about the report does the first paragraph answer?
  A When did people write this report? _____
  B What parts of life is the report about? _____
  C Which ideas are the most interesting? _____
  D Who gave their ideas for the report? _____
  E Which jobs will be most important? _____

2 What ideas about the future are in the rest of the text?
  A There will be cities under the ground. _____
  B We will live under the sea. _____
  C We won't have any walls inside our homes. _____
  D We will move homes from place to place. _____
  E There will be more hotels in the world. _____
  F Nobody will go to the beach on holiday. _____
  G We will go on holiday to the moon. _____

LISTENING

PREPARE FOR THE EXAM

Listening Part 4

1 For each question, choose the correct answer.

08

1 You will hear two friends talking on the way to school. What did the girl forget to do before she left home?
A find something
B turn something off
C wash some things up

2 You will hear a girl talking about some train tickets. What is she explaining?
A how they got the wrong ones
B why it was not possible to get any
C how difficult it was to get them

3 You will hear a boy and his mother talking about tomorrow evening. Who does the boy need to talk to?
A his brother
B staff at the restaurant
C someone he plays basketball with

4 You will hear a boy telling his friend about breaking something. What is he worried about?
A his grandma's feelings
B telling his mother
C how to repair it

5 You will hear a woman talking about the weather. How will it change next week?
A It will be colder.
B It will be wetter.
C It will be windier.

EXAM TIPS

- Each question is a different conversation between different people.
- Before you listen, read all the questions and the answers carefully.

WRITING   Making predictions about your life

1 Read the explanation and the website message. Then match the parts of the text A–D to the questions below.

1 Will you be married or single and will you have any children?
2 How old will you be?
3 Where will you live?
4 What will your job be?

This is a message on a website from a young man to himself in the future. People write to themselves on this website, and the website sends them the message at a time they choose in the future.

Home	About	Messages

Hello future me!

This is how I think your life will be in 2040.

(A) You will be 40 years old in 2040. **(B)** You will live in a nice flat in Barcelona. **(C)** You will be a chef in a big restaurant in Barcelona, too. **(D)** You may be married and you may also have some children.

Are my predictions right?

Jorge

2 Write to the future you in 2040 and answer the questions in Exercise 1.

9 SPORTS, GAMES AND ACTIVITIES

1 Which activities are they talking about? Choose the correct words.

My parents don't like me looking at a screen for a long time, so I can play these for only an hour a day.

4 Alistair: **A** puzzles **B** video games

These are much more fun than other exercise. I love the music our teachers use.

1 Ursula: **A** dance classes **B** card games

I do this every winter with my family. It's really exciting because you go down the mountain so quickly.

5 Kai: **A** climbing **B** skiing

I practise doing this every day. The colour of my belt shows the level I'm at.

2 Tony: **A** diving **B** karate

I play this with my cousin every time we visit him in England! One player throws the ball and the other player tries to hit the ball with a bat.

6 Vladimir: **A** cricket **B** golf

My sisters and I play these together at home when we can't go outside. I love winning!

3 Eren: **A** fitness classes **B** board games

I really enjoy racket sports. That's why I started doing this.

7 Patrick: **A** badminton **B** skateboarding

2 Match the descriptions to the activities.

1	card games	....	**a** When you do these, you think a lot because you have to find answers.
2	climbing	....	**b** When you do these, you usually have to listen to a teacher.
3	diving	....	**c** You can do this in a swimming pool, the sea or a lake.
4	fishing	....	**d** You usually play this sport outside with a small white ball.
5	golf	....	**e** When you do this, you stand or jump on something and it moves.
6	puzzles	....	**f** When you do this, you might catch something to eat.
7	skateboarding	....	**g** You usually play these inside with friends or family.
8	fitness classes	....	**h** You can do this outside going up rocks, or inside going up high walls.

GRAMMAR

must, mustn't, have to and don't have to

1 Match the sentence halves.

1 We must ....
2 We mustn't ....
3 We don't have to ....

a buy our books because the school gives us them.
b fill in a form before we can join the sports club.
c use our mobile phones in lessons.

2 Complete the sentences with *must, mustn't* or *don't have to.*

1 We .... wear a uniform for sports lessons. We wear our own sports clothes.
2 At our school, we have to wear a uniform. We .... wear jeans or T-shirts.
3 We .... walk in the corridor. Running is dangerous.
4 We .... take our books back to the library so other students can read them.
5 We .... talk in the classroom. We have to be quiet.
6 We .... go to homework club but lots of people do.

3 Correct the mistakes in three of the sentences. Which two are correct?

1 You have not to bring anything because the teacher will give you what you need.

2 It will be cold, so you must wear warm clothes!

3 You mustn't spend so much time on the internet.

4 Tomorrow night you must come to my house. To get to my house you had to take the number 15 bus.

5 You don't must bring anything because I've got everything.

4 Write sentences about James. Then complete the table and write sentences about you.

What did you have to do when you were younger?

	James	You
do a sport I didn't like	✓	
eat everything on my plate at meal times	✗	
go to bed at 7.30	✓	
wear my brother's old clothes	✗	
walk to school with one of my parents	✓	

James
0 *He had to do a sport he didn't like.*
1 ....
2 ....
3 ....
4 ....

You
1 ....
2 ....
3 ....
4 ....
5 ....

VOCABULARY — Sports vocabulary

1 Complete the blog with the words in the box.

champions   fans   prize   professional
take part   tournaments

FOOTBALL CRAZY

My friends and I all love football. We're ¹ .... of Manchester United, Arsenal and Liverpool football clubs. Every week we watch the matches in all the big football competitions. We try to answer the question 'Who will be the ² .... this year?' We don't always agree! We love watching the big ³ .... like the World Cup, too. We also ⁴ .... in football eSports competitions online. I'm not very good at them but one of my friends is. He won a ⁵ .... in a competition last month. He wants to be a ⁶ .... eSports football player when he's older.

2 Use the words in the box to write the professions of the famous people. If you're not sure, look online.

~~dive~~   golf   photograph   run   sing   ski   swim

0 Tom Daley (UK): *diver*
1 Michael Phelps (USA): ....
2 Irem Derici (Turkey): ....
3 Tina Maze (Slovenia): ....
4 Usain Bolt (Jamaica): ....
5 Sebastião Salgado (Brazil): ....
6 Jon Rahm (Spain): ....

SPORTS, GAMES AND ACTIVITIES 37

1 Read the text quickly. What is Mark Durant's job? _____

Becoming a **professional gamer**

If you're a very good video game player, perhaps you could become a professional gamer. But it's not easy.

You have to love playing games, and you have to spend a lot of time playing them. The first thing to do is to decide what game you want to play as a professional. Then you have to spend as much time as possible playing it, and learning everything you can about it.

It's important to play the game against better players. You have to find out how they play differently from you. And you must practise by working hard on the things that are difficult for you. Also, don't try to improve too many things all at the same time.

But practising on your own will not be enough. Soon, you must join a group of gamers. It's the only way to become a great player. Talking with others about how you play is really good for your game. Learn the rules of the group before you join – each group is different.

Taking part in tournaments is important too, starting with small local tournaments. It's a great way to see if you play well or not. Later, when you play better, you should enter bigger tournaments with more players taking part.

Mark Durant, a professional gamer, says it's very important to stay fit, too. Sitting at a screen all day is very bad for you. So last year while he was travelling to tournaments, he designed and made some exercise videos. Gamers can use them in their hotel rooms because there's no time for doing fitness classes or other activities.

Do you think you could do this as a job?

 PREPARE FOR THE EXAM

Reading Part 3

2 For each question, choose the correct answer.

1 What advice does the writer give in the first paragraph?
A Try a few games and spend time playing them.
B Choose one game and just practise playing that.
C Learn all about a game before you play it.

2 The writer says you should play against better players to learn
A things you must not do.
B other ways of playing.
C how to do everything better than them.

3 What does the writer say about joining a group of gamers?
A It's a good idea for some people.
B If you want to play better, you have to do it.
C Some groups are more helpful than others.

4 The writer says that taking part in tournaments helps you
A find out how good you are.
B play better more quickly.
C meet other players.

5 What did Mark Durant do last year?
A He made some exercise videos.
B He went to fitness classes.
C He opened a hotel for gamers.

 EXAM TIPS

- The questions are in the same order as the information in the text.
- Compare the questions and options to the text carefully.

LISTENING

1 Listen to two friends, Matt and Emma, talking about Matt's golf class. Are the sentences right (✓) or wrong (✗)?

1 Matt is telling Emma about his golf class for the first time. ....

2 Matt is trying to stop Emma going to his golf class. ....

3 Emma asks Matt for information about the golf class. ....

4 Emma will probably go to the golf class. ....

2 Listen again and write one word or number for each answer.

1 The golf class is on .... each week now.

2 Emma must book .... of the golf classes.

3 Emma won't pay for her .... golf class.

4 The teacher worked in the past as a ....

5 Emma will probably .... from her home to the golf class.

6 Matt bought his own golf .... for the class.

7 Emma will .... the teacher to ask her about joining the class.

WRITING — Posting an opinion on a blog

1 Read the blog posts about eSports and answer the questions.

1 Does bluediamond agree with the blog writer?

2 Draw a star (*) in the text to show the beginning of bluediamond's opinion.

> I think eSports should never be part of the Olympics. They are not really sports because you don't have to be fit to do them.
>
> **Do you agree that eSports should never be part of the Olympics? Join the conversation.**
>
> ---
>
>
> 23rd April 19:01
> In your blog, you say that eSports should never be part of the Olympics. You think eSports are not really sports because you don't have to be fit to do them.
> I don't agree. It's not true that you don't have to be fit. eSports gamers have to play for many hours without any breaks. The best players eat healthily and do exercise every day. eSports should be part of the Olympics!
> **bluediamond**

2 Read the blog and write a response with your own opinion about mind sports.

> I think it's a good idea to have mind sports (chess, board games, card games, etc.) in the Olympics. Thinking and using your brain is important in every sport.
>
> **Do you agree that it's a good idea to have mind sports in the Olympics? Join the conversation.**

....

....

....

....

....

10 USEFUL WEBSITES

1 Complete the sentences with the correct form of the words in the box.

| classmate | contact | guest | member |
| neighbour | relative | | |

1 Last week our new _____ moved in next door to us. They're from Hungary.
2 Do you have to pay to be a _____ of the online film club you told me about?
3 The _____ staying with us at the moment are old friends of my mum's.
4 How many _____ do you have in your phone?
5 I don't have any _____ living near me in London because both my parents' families live in Russia.
6 I know Henry because he was a _____ at my old school, but he was never really a good friend.

2 Choose the correct words to complete the sentences.

1 We talk on the phone every day now so we've become really _____ friends.
  A old   B close
2 His number is not in my _____ list so I can't phone him.
  A relatives   B contacts
3 My _____ moved to a new school last month. I really miss her.
  A best friend B penfriend
4 Sara and Isabel are _____ of my mum's. They met at work 15 years ago.
  A old friends B classmates
5 My _____ is teaching me Italian. I'm going to meet him for the first time when he comes to stay with me in Wales next month.
  A neighbour   B penfriend

1 Choose the correct verb forms to complete the sentences.

1 I finished *doing* / *to do* my homework and I went to the cinema.
2 My sister enjoys *playing* / *to play* the piano.
3 I need *learning* / *to learn* computer code because I want to create my own website.
4 My friend wanted *buying* / *to buy* a laptop, but they were too expensive.
5 Jack doesn't mind *studying* / *study* for exams, but Ronnie hates it.
6 *Sleeping* / *To sleep* for 7–8 hours a night helps you stay healthy.

2 Match the sentence halves.

1 I tried   _____
2 My brother loves   _____
3 I'm thinking of   _____
4 My sister hopes   _____
5 Jay's worried about   _____

a failing his maths exam. He says he needs to study more.
b to play for the school basketball team next year.
c to make a pizza for my family, but it didn't go very well. It was horrible!
d meeting friends every weekend. They always have a really good time.
e studying Russian next term. We can choose between Russian and French.

3 Complete the sentences with the gerund or the infinitive form of the verbs in brackets.

1 I'm planning _____ (live) in New York when I leave school.
2 Sara doesn't mind _____ (see) the film for a second time.
3 You need _____ (study) really hard if you want to do well in your exams.
4 I'm really afraid of _____ (lose) my phone. I use it for everything.
5 My sister decided _____ (go) to university in Istanbul.
6 _____ (listen) to music while I study helps me a lot.

4 Tick (✓) the correct sentences.

1 A I'm not very interested in seeing this film.
  B I'm not very interested in see this film.
2 A The class starts on Monday. Don't forget to bring your things.
  B The class starts on Monday. Don't forget bring your things.
3 A I like reading and listening to music. Swim is also good.
  B I like reading and listening to music. Swimming is also good.
4 A Thank you very much for invite me to your party.
  B Thank you very much for inviting me to your party.
5 A At the music club we sing and learn to play the guitar.
  B At the music club we sing and learn playing the guitar.

1 Choose the correct words to complete the sentences.

1 Click on the *menu / link* to find out more about saving the planet.
2 The *web / blog* was invented by Tim Berners-Lee in 1989.
3 Amazon is a very popular *message board / site*.
4 My sister writes a really interesting *blog / menu* about video games.
5 There are lots of pages on the site, so use the *menu / web* to find the page you want.
6 My brother likes writing comments on *links / message boards*.

2 Find six internet verbs.

x	s	u	p	l	o	a	d	r
p	a	z	n	t	g	k	q	e
o	v	q	i	w	v	m	p	c
s	e	s	e	a	r	c	h	o
t	r	a	n	w	v	m	d	r
r	d	o	w	n	l	o	a	d

3 Complete the sentences with the correct form of the verbs in Exercise 2.

1 I forgot to _____ the file and lost all my homework.
2 Chiara _____ her songs to YouTube last week and now she's got a lot of fans of her music.
3 Yuri likes _____ messages on message boards.
4 We _____ a great new film onto my computer last night. We're going to watch it this weekend.
5 Bartek _____ his friend singing a song and sent it to his other friends.
6 I usually find the information I need when I _____ for it online.

READING

1 Read the article quickly. What kind of videos are popular on YouTube?

YouTube

1 YouTube is the name of one of the most popular sites on the **(1)** .... People watch and share millions of videos on the site. A young American man **(2)** .... the first video onto YouTube in April 2005. It was a short film of his friend at the zoo.

2 Now, every month, visitors to the site watch about 6 billion (thousand million) hours of YouTube videos. This is **(3)** .... because it has so many different sorts of videos. When you **(4)** .... for a topic online, there is usually at least one **(5)** .... to a YouTube video on the list of sites to click on. After each YouTube video, you can **(6)** .... a message, telling other people what you think of it.

3 The most popular kind of videos on YouTube are music videos. Every time you look on the site, the numbers change, but in December 2017, the most popular music video was of a song called *Despacito* by Luis Fonsi. More than 4 billion people watched it before the end of 2017!

4 Funny videos of children and pets are also very popular on YouTube. One of the most popular is called *Charlie Bit Me*. It has a young boy, Harry, and his baby brother, Charlie, in it. The baby hurts the boy a little, and then laughs. Howard Davies-Carr, the father of the boys, made the video in 2007, and put it on YouTube for their grandfather to see. Millions of people loved watching the video and thought it was funny. In 2017, Howard made another video of his two sons saying the same words.

✓ PREPARE FOR THE EXAM

Reading Part 4

2 For each question, choose the correct answer.

1	**A** menu	**B** blog	**C** web
2	**A** uploaded	**B** joined	**C** contacted
3	**A** finally	**B** probably	**C** immediately
4	**A** record	**B** download	**C** search
5	**A** link	**B** way	**C** app
6	**A** chat	**B** post	**C** make

✓ EXAM TIPS

• Try each word (A, B and C) in the space.
• After you choose your answer, read the whole sentence carefully to make sure it's correct.

3 Read paragraphs 3 and 4 of the text again. Then complete the sentences with one word or number.

1 .... videos are more popular than any other kind of video on YouTube.
2 The video of Luis Fonsi was the most popular YouTube video in .... 2017.
3 In *Charlie Bit Me,* Charlie's brother is called ....
4 Charlie's father wanted Charlie's .... to see the video.
5 Howard made a second video of the boys in ....

LISTENING

🔊 **1** Listen to two friends, Cathy and Stuart, talking about a website. Write *C* (Cathy) or *S* (Stuart).
10

0 ..*S*.. is listening to music when they meet.
1 .... gives information about a website.
2 .... wants to find out about the website.
3 .... thinks the cost after 30 days is expensive.
4 .... has the idea about their band uploading a song.
5 .... doesn't want their band to upload a song at the moment.

🔊 **2** Listen again. Are the sentences right (✓) or wrong (✗)?
10

1 Stuart is listening to his favourite band.
2 The website only has very new music on it.
3 The music on the site is all Australian.
4 Stuart is not paying to download music from the site now.
5 Stuart thinks some of the music on the site is strange.
6 There are about 100,000 videos on the site.

WRITING An email

1 Read the penfriends' emails and the list of online activities below. Then number the things Hakan does most 1–3 (1 = most, 3 = least).

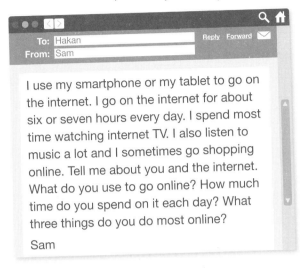

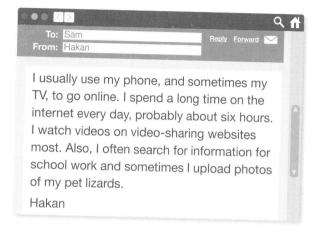

To: Hakan
From: Sam
Reply Forward

I use my smartphone or my tablet to go on the internet. I go on the internet for about six or seven hours every day. I spend most time watching internet TV. I also listen to music a lot and I sometimes go shopping online. Tell me about you and the internet. What do you use to go online? How much time do you spend on it each day? What three things do you do most online?

Sam

To: Sam
From: Hakan
Reply Forward

I usually use my phone, and sometimes my TV, to go online. I spend a long time on the internet every day, probably about six hours. I watch videos on video-sharing websites most. Also, I often search for information for school work and sometimes I upload photos of my pet lizards.

Hakan

What do you do most on the internet?	Sam	Hakan	You
• send and get emails			
• read the news			
• watch internet TV	1		
• search for information			
• watch videos on video-sharing websites			
• play games online			
• listen to music	2		
• chat			
• upload videos / photos, etc.			
• shop	3		

2 Number the three things <u>you</u> do most on the internet.

✓ PREPARE FOR THE EXAM

Writing Part 6

3 Read the email from your English friend, Sam.

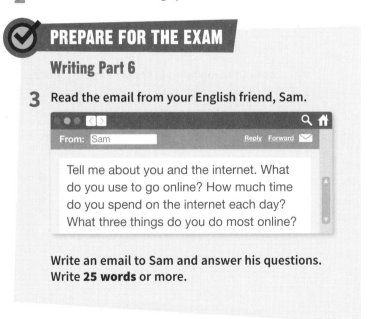

From: Sam
Reply Forward

Tell me about you and the internet. What do you use to go online? How much time do you spend on the internet each day? What three things do you do most online?

Write an email to Sam and answer his questions. Write **25 words** or more.

 EXAM TIPS

• Always check your grammar, spelling and punctuation.
• Make sure you answer the three questions.

11 CITY LIVING

1 **Look at the photo below. Answer the questions with *yes* or *no*.**

1 Can you see a fountain in the photo?
2 Can you see a cathedral in the photo?
3 Can you see a statue in the photo?
4 Can you see a mosque in the photo?
5 Can you see a stadium in the photo?
6 Can you see a skyscraper in the photo?
7 Can you see a temple in the photo?

2 **Match the sentences to the places.**

1 When you are travelling in another country, you can go here for help.
2 People go here to see the work of famous artists.
3 This is a piece of art. It is usually made of stone or metal and looks like a person or animal.
4 A king or queen's family may live in this.
5 People go here to see a football match.
6 People go here to find lots of different kinds of things to buy.
7 This is an area with the original houses and buildings in a modern city.

a a palace
b a stadium
c a shopping area
d an art gallery
e a statue
f an embassy
g old town

GRAMMAR   Determiners

1 **Choose the correct words to complete the descriptions of cities.**

1 This is one of *a / the* most beautiful cities in Europe. It's *a / the* capital of the Netherlands and it's famous for its bridges and museums. It's *a / the* great place for riding a bike.
2 This is one of *a / the* biggest cities in the United States of America. Tourists come here to see *a / the* Statue of Liberty and visit art galleries like the Museum of Modern Art. The city is called *all / both* 'the city that never sleeps' and 'The Big Apple'.
3 This city is in the United Kingdom. There are many reasons to visit this city – the parks, museums and shops are *all / both* excellent. *Another / Other* reason visitors come here is to go to the theatre. The Olympic Games were here in 2012.
4 This city is Russia's capital. It has *the / a* very famous square in its centre. It is called Red Square. There are some beautiful cathedrals here, as well as lots of *other / another* interesting buildings.

2 **Read the descriptions in Exercise 1 again. What are the cities?**

1 ....   3 ....
2 ....   4 ....

3 **Correct the mistakes in three of the sentences. Which two are correct?**

1 I live on the Black Street at number 10.

2 Vancouver has both mountains and beaches.

3 All the students were waiting to go into the new museum.

4 We had an sports competition today.

5 I want a penfriend in other country.

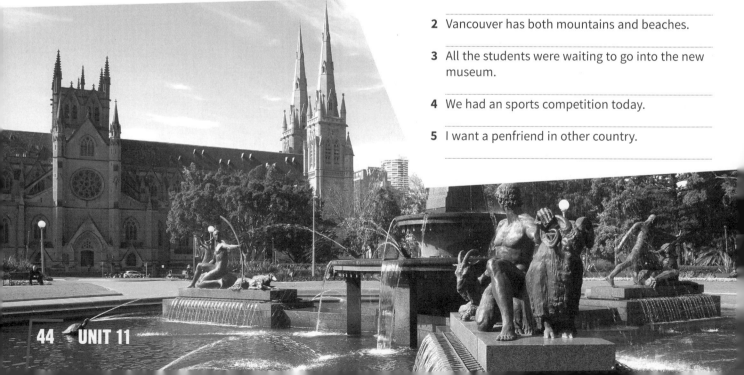

4 Complete the article with the words in the box. You can use some words more than once.

a	all	both	the

CARDIFF

Cardiff is ¹ _____ capital city of Wales. It's not ² _____ large city, but it's ³ _____ biggest one in Wales. Cardiff is very friendly. It's ⁴ _____ good city to visit because there's lots to do there. It's by the sea and it has parks, shops and restaurants. It also has ⁵ _____ theatres and stadiums. ⁶ _____ the road signs in Cardiff are in two languages: Welsh and English. ⁷ _____ these languages are spoken in Cardiff, but ⁸ _____ first language of most people there is English.

1 Replace the <u>underlined</u> parts of the sentences with the words in the box.

~~food~~	furniture	information	jewellery
luggage	money	staff	wildlife

Students:
do not eat your <u>sandwiches or anything else</u> in the classroom.

0 _____food_____

Please leave your <u>suitcases</u> at the reception desk.

1 _____

Broken glass can hurt <u>animals and birds</u> in this park: please take your empty bottles home.

2 _____

Go online
for further <u>details</u> about concerts at the stadium.

3 _____

You can use <u>coins</u> or bank cards in these car park machines.

4 _____

Our <u>shop assistants</u> are happy to help.

5 _____

All the silver <u>necklaces and rings</u> on this shelf are now **HALF PRICE**

6 _____

If you move the <u>desks and chairs</u> in this classroom, please put everything back at the end of the lesson.

7 _____

2 Complete the sentences with the pairs of words.

(food, meal) (homework, projects)
(news, articles) (traffic, car) (batteries, electricity)

1 I've got to do two _____ for my _____ this week.
2 When I go out to a restaurant for a _____, I usually have Italian _____.
3 We had to turn off the _____ while Dad repaired the cooker last night. The _____ in both my phone and my tablet were empty at the end of the evening.
4 I never come to college by _____ because the _____ in the city is so bad in the morning.
5 You should read the _____ on this site today. There are three really interesting _____ about city life for young adults.

1 Read the notices and message and <u>underline</u> the places in a city.

1

Staff in every area of the stadium are happy to answer visitors' questions

2

USE FREE INTERNET

AND BUY FRESH SNACKS AT THE PALACE'S CAFÉ

OPEN 10—4

3

Art gallery tours with one of our artists *every Saturday!*

4

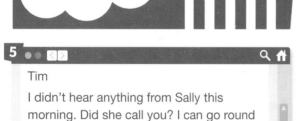

Visiting the **skyscraper**

Too cloudy to see the view? Get **free tickets** for another day.

5

Tim

I didn't hear anything from Sally this morning. Did she call you? I can go round to her house later. Let me know.

Jackie

6

MUSEUM TOURS

Check the timetable on our website, then buy your tickets at the museum reception desk.

Reading Part 1

2 For each question, choose the correct answer.

1 What does this notice tell visitors they can do?
  A go into all parts of the stadium
  B ask a stadium worker when they want to know something
  C enter some areas of the stadium only with a member of staff

2 A You have to pay to use the internet in the café after ten o'clock.
  B You get special offers on the café food when you visit the palace.
  C You can go online and have something to eat in the café until four o'clock.

3 What will happen each week?
  A An artist will go around the gallery with visitors.
  B There will be a different artist's work at the gallery.
  C Visitors can watch an artist working.

4 A In cloudy weather it is free to go up the skyscraper.
  B If you cannot see anything from the skyscraper, you can visit again without paying.
  C You can stay longer at the top of the skyscraper when it's cloudy.

5 Why is Jackie writing to Tim?
  A She can't contact one of their friends.
  B Tim isn't answering the telephone.
  C She wants Tim to visit Sally.

6 A Pay for tickets online before collecting them at the museum.
  B Find out when the tours will happen before you visit the museum.
  C Ask at the reception desk when you can buy tickets online.

EXAM TIPS

- Quickly read the short texts and think about where you might see them.
- Compare each answer (A, B and C) to the text before you choose the correct one.

LISTENING

1 Listen to someone talking about a sports stadium and tick (✓) the correct sentences.

The speaker
1 tells you what's going to happen in one month.
2 gives you information about when the stadium's open.
3 is talking to stadium staff.
4 wants you to go to the stadium.

2 Listen again and choose the correct answers.

Harlake Stadium

5 January

New Year's family party – the city's biggest party!
Family of four: £50. Includes for each person a
¹ *meal / snack*, music, games and dancing.

11 January

Music concert with top band Money Talks
The band will perform songs from their number one album ² *Money / Honey*. Tickets cost ³ *£43 / £45* online.

14 January

Professor Clinton Richards is talking about his new book *Know Everything*. The first ⁴ *five / thirty-five* people to buy a ticket will meet Professor Richards in the stadium's ⁵ *restaurant / cinema*.

18–21 January

Tennis tournament – 18th and 19th for players ⁶ *under / over* 16, and 20th and 21st for ⁷ *under 16s / young adults*. Tickets cost £10 every day of the tournament.

WRITING — Formal and informal messages

1 Read the three messages and answer the questions.

1 Which message from Deniz is more formal: the one to Maisie or to Mr Greg? _____
2 Which words and / or phrases show you it is more formal? (Circle) these in the text.
3 Which words and / or phrases in the other message show you it is more informal? Underline these in the text.

> **From: Deniz:**
> Hi Maisie, can you tell me the name of the book we have to buy for our science class? I didn't write it in my notebook. Thanks! Deniz

> **From: Maisie:**
> Hi Deniz, sorry, I can't help you. I wasn't at school last week, when Mr Greg told the class. Can you tell me when you know, please? Maisie

To: Mr Greg   Reply Forward ✉
From: Deniz Mehmetoglu

Dear Mr Greg,
Please could you tell me the name of the science book we need to buy? I'm afraid I did not write it in my notebook.
Deniz Mehmetoglu

2 Yesterday your teacher, Mrs Gibson, told your class the dates of the school trip to Paris. You were not at school.

Write two emails asking for this information.
• one to a friend
• one to Mrs Gibson

To: Reply Forward ✉

To: Mrs Gibson   Reply Forward ✉

12 FILMS

VOCABULARY — Types of film

1 Complete the types of film with the missing vowels.

1. _ c t _ _ _ n
2. _ n _ m _ t _ d
3. _ d v _ n t _ r _
4. m _ _ s _ c _ l
5. s c _ _ n c _ f _ c t _ _ n

2 What kind of films are these? Put the letters in the correct order.

1. *La La Land* (clumasi) _____
2. *Bilal: A New Breed of Hero* (timneada imlf) _____
3. *Transformers: The Last Knight* (cicnese infocit) _____
4. *Baby Driver* (lertihlr) _____
5. *Summer 1993* (radam) _____

3 Choose the correct answers. Sometimes more than one answer is possible.

1. When you watch this kind of film, you will probably be frightened.
   - **A** a horror film
   - **B** a musical
   - **C** a thriller
2. Songs are an important part of this kind of film.
   - **A** a comedy
   - **B** an adventure film
   - **C** a musical
3. This kind of film is usually very exciting.
   - **A** an adventure film
   - **B** a comedy
   - **C** an action film
4. This kind of film uses moving drawings.
   - **A** a drama
   - **B** a science fiction film
   - **C** an animated film
5. You hear real actors in this kind of film, but you don't actually see them.
   - **A** a horror film
   - **B** an animated film
   - **C** a musical
6. This kind of film is funny.
   - **A** a thriller
   - **B** an action film
   - **C** a comedy
7. This kind of film tells a story about people's feelings and problems.
   - **A** an animated film
   - **B** a horror film
   - **C** a drama

GRAMMAR — Relative pronouns *who*, *which*, *that*

1 Choose the correct relative pronoun.

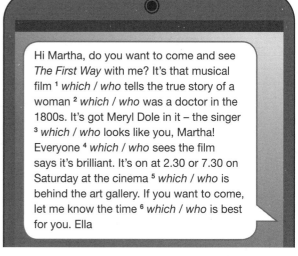

Hi Martha, do you want to come and see *The First Way* with me? It's that musical film ¹ *which / who* tells the true story of a woman ² *which / who* was a doctor in the 1800s. It's got Meryl Dole in it – the singer ³ *which / who* looks like you, Martha! Everyone ⁴ *which / who* sees the film says it's brilliant. It's on at 2.30 or 7.30 on Saturday at the cinema ⁵ *which / who* is behind the art gallery. If you want to come, let me know the time ⁶ *which / who* is best for you. Ella

2 Put the words in the correct order to make sentences. Which sentence matches the photo below?

1. has / which / The Arts Centre cinema / large seats / really comfortable / are
   _____
2. films / three hours / don't like / I / that / longer than / are
   _____
3. actors / the stars of / are usually / who / are / very fit / action films
   _____
4. the actor / in the Avengers films / that / is / Scarlett Johansson / plays Black Widow
   _____
5. likes / my oldest brother / the only person in our family / is / horror films / who
   _____

sentence _____

3 Tick (✓) the correct sentences.

1 **A** Yesterday I bought a black jacket and a pair of jeans who are blue.

B Yesterday I bought a black jacket and a pair of jeans which are blue.

2 **A** When you come here we can go swimming in the lake who is near my house.

B When you come here we can go swimming in the lake that is near my house.

3 **A** Last Saturday I bought a white skirt which cost 40 dollars.

B Last Saturday I bought a white skirt which it cost 40 dollars.

4 **A** My favourite birthday present is my bike. It was Jim gave it to me.

B My favourite birthday present is my bike. It was Jim who gave it to me.

5 **A** You need to bring three pencils and the book that the teacher will give you.

B You need to bring three pencils and the book who the teacher will give you.

1 Choose the correct words to complete the sentences.

1 Would you like to go to the cinema *when / while* I come back from work, Lucas?

2 There's a cinema in my town *if / where* they give you a free piece of cake during the film.

3 I don't like watching films, *so / that* I never go to the cinema.

4 I enjoy listening to music *where / while* I'm reading books for school.

5 *While / If* I finish my project soon, I'll watch that thriller with you.

6 Pablo says *if / that* the musical is on twice on Saturdays.

7 My brother doesn't enjoy watching comedy films *or / when* musicals with me because I laugh and sing too loudly.

2 Complete the sentences with the words in brackets.

0 I go to the cinema ____*when*____ it's raining. I go to the old cinema, ____*where*____ the snacks are cheap. (where, when)

1 I think _____ musicals are terrible _____ the actors aren't brilliant singers. (that, if)

2 I was really scared in the film _____ the boy suddenly fell off the horse. I closed my eyes _____ he was running through the forest. (while, when)

3 It's difficult to enjoy a film _____ you're sitting behind someone who's really tall. I always sit at the front of the cinema, _____ nobody can sit in front of me. (where, when)

4 My grandma told me _____ she went to the cinema nearly every evening _____ she was a younger woman. (when, that)

5 We could go and see that police drama tonight _____ you want to, or we could go on Thursday, _____ that action film will be on. (if, when)

6 I'm not going out this evening _____ I might watch TV _____ I might go to bed early. (or, so)

1 Read the text quickly. How many days was the film festival?

....

What people said about Plymouth Film Festival at the Arts Centre

William

In June, I went to the Plymouth Film Festival for the first time. I stayed with my aunt in Plymouth city centre, and I was there for the whole weekend of the festival. I had a great time. Everything, from the films to the food available in restaurants and cafés near the Arts Centre, was exactly right. But I especially loved the short animated films and the comedies. I can't wait to see more next June.

Milo

The Plymouth Film Festival is always a wonderful weekend. All the people who work to make the festival happen are so friendly and really love the films they show. This year it was difficult to choose which films to see because there were so many different kinds, from horror films to musicals. I wanted to see many more but I didn't have time. The best thing that I saw was the winner of the student's prize. It was a short drama called *Uncle*.

Freddie

There were lots of good things about Plymouth Film Festival. The only problem was that it was too short. For me, no other film festival is as good as this one, and I'd like it to be for two weeks instead of two days. One great thing was making new friends after every film – we all loved the films and talked for hours about them. I'd like to go back to Plymouth soon – what a great place. I really want to learn more about its history.

PREPARE FOR THE EXAM

Reading Part 2

2 **For each question, choose the correct answer. Write *W* for William, *M* for Milo or *F* for Freddie.**

1 Which person is interested in finding out more about the city where the festival happened? ....

2 Which person is planning to go to the film festival again? ....

3 Which person thinks the festival is better than any other film festival? ....

4 Which person enjoyed meeting other people at the festival? ....

5 Which person says there was a wide variety of films at the festival? ....

6 Which person says the festival was perfect in every way? ....

7 Which person says which film was his favourite at the festival? ....

EXAM TIPS

- The text and the questions say the same information using different words.
- After you choose your answer, read the other texts again to make sure they are both wrong.

PREPARE FOR THE EXAM

Listening Part 3

1 For each question, choose the correct answer.

🔊 **You will hear Marina telling her friend Lucas about a film she is going to make.**
12

1 Who will Marina spend Friday evening with?
   A her family   **B** Lucas and Sarah   **C** some classmates

2 The students who will take part in the competition are from
   A just Marina's school.   **B** all parts of the country.   **C** several countries.

3 The film that Marina is planning is a
   A thriller.   **B** comedy.   **C** musical.

4 When will Marina know if her film is the competition winner?
   A on 12th June   **B** on 19th June   **C** on 30th June

5 Where is the film festival?
   A at the Arts Centre
   B at the old cinema
   C at the film school

EXAM TIPS

- You will hear all three answers (A, B and C) mentioned in the conversation, but only one is right.
- The first time you listen, choose the correct answer. The second time you listen, check your answers.

An invitation to a club

1 Read the book club poster and the invitation from Anya. Then complete the answers to the questions.

1 Where is the book club?
in ....

2 What time does the book club start?
at ....

3 What's the title of the book that club members are reading this month?
....

4 What day is the book club?
on ....

5 What kind of book are the club members reading this month?
a ....

6 What time does the book club finish?
at ....

7 What does Anya think of the book?
it's ....

2 Read the film club poster and answer the questions. Don't forget the prepositions (*in*, *at*, *on*) in some of the answers.

1 Where is the film club?
....

2 What time does the film club start?
....

3 What's the title of the film that club members will watch next month?
....

4 What day is the book club?
....

5 What kind of film will the club members watch next month?
....

6 What time does the film club finish?
....

> When: first Friday of every month 2.30–4 pm
> Place: Art Room 3
> Next month's film: animated film *Spirited Away*

3 Write to a friend and invite them to the College Film Club. Include the points below.

- when it is
- what time it starts and finishes
- the title of next month's film and what kind of film it is
- what you think of the film (you watched it three years ago)
- ask your friend to respond to the invitation

....
....
....
....
....
....
....
....
....
....
....
....
....
....
....
....
....

Teenagers' **Book Club**

📖 **When: first Monday of every month 4–5.30 pm**

📖 **Place: the town library**

📖 **This month's book: Harriet Streep's new thriller *Leave before midnight***

Hi Priti

Would you like to come to the Teenagers' Book Club with me? It's on the first Monday of every month in the town library. It starts at four o'clock and finishes at 5.30. This month we're reading *Leave before midnight,* which is a thriller by Harriet Streep. I'm reading it really quickly because it's so exciting. Let me know if you want to come!

Anya

13 LIFE EXPERIENCES

1 Choose the nouns which <u>don't</u> go with the verbs and phrases. Sometimes more than one answer is possible.

0 climb …
A a mountain **B** (the sea) **C** a tree

1 kayak down …
A a river **B** a cave **C** a hill

2 pick …
A wild fruit **B** wild eggs **C** wild birds

3 camp …
A in a forest **B** under the stars **C** in a hotel

4 play in the …
A sea **B** snow **C** sky

5 explore …
A an animal **B** a forest **C** a cave

6 look for … at the beach
A fossils **B** fruit **C** flowers

7 track wild …
A fruit **B** animals **C** fossils

8 try … climbing
A mountain **B** forest **C** rock

9 record …
A a tree **B** a cave **C** birdsong

2 Answer the questions.

1 Which activities in Exercise 1 can you do near where you live?

2 Which activities are you planning to do this year?

3 Which activities do you think are dangerous?

GRAMMAR Present perfect with *ever* and *never*

1 Complete the sentences with the past participle form of the verbs in the box.

camp	explore	listen
play	visit	watch

1 I've never _____ to jazz.

2 My parents have never _____ me play in a tennis tournament.

3 Richard has never _____ me in my new home.

4 I have never _____ with my family because we don't have a tent.

5 Emily has never _____ a musical instrument.

6 I came to this part of the city once before, but I've never really _____ it.

2 Write questions in the present perfect.

0 talk / famous person
Have you ever talked to a famous person?

1 kayak / down a river
_____?

2 pick / an orange from a tree
_____?

3 play / the drums
_____?

4 watch / a really scary film
_____?

5 climb / a mountain
_____?

6 camp / next to a river or lake
_____?

7 try / horse riding
_____?

3 Answer the questions in Exercise 2 for you. Use short answers. For your *yes* answers, write when you did this.

0 *Yes, I have. I talked to a famous writer two years ago.*
1
2
3
4
5
6
7

4 Correct the mistakes in three of the sentences. Which two are correct?

1 I've never joined a climbing club.

_____

2 I have to tell you that this have never happened before.

_____

3 Have you ever cooked a meal outside, under the stars?

_____

4 Ayrton Senna was the best Formula 1 driver that have ever lived.

_____

5 I really like *Call of Juarez*. It's the best video game that I have never played.

_____

VOCABULARY Past participles

1 Find the past participles of the verbs in the box.

be	break	eat	fly	grow
have	make	meet	ride	
send	sleep	swim		

s	e	d	g	r	o	w	n	d
t	a	o	l	h	a	d	b	i
e	a	t	e	n	b	s	e	g
p	g	r	s	t	r	w	e	r
m	l	n	t	k	o	s	n	l
e	d	x	v	m	k	e	s	d
t	m	a	d	e	e	n	l	d
b	w	c	m	u	n	t	e	e
l	s	w	u	m	n	c	p	n
f	l	o	w	n	p	f	t	t

2 Complete the conversation with the questions A–E.

Rob: Hi, Anna.
Anna: Hi, Rob. What are you reading?
Rob: Oh, it's a questionnaire on a website called timetotry.com. [1] _____
Anna: No, I haven't. Can you ask me some of the questions?
Rob: OK. The first question is: [2] _____
Anna: No, never, but my parents have lots in our garden.
Rob: Really? Here's the next question. [3] _____
Anna: Yes, last week during a boring drama about a man and his motorbike.
Rob: [4] _____
Anna: No, I haven't, but I'd like to. What's the next question?
Rob: [5] _____
Anna: Yes! Once I wrote an email to a friend but put Mum's address on it – Mum thought it was funny, but I didn't!
Rob: Oh no!

A Have you ever ridden one?
B Have you ever grown your own vegetables?
C Have you ever sent a message to the wrong person?
D Have you ever been on that site?
E Have you ever slept during a film at the cinema?

3 Write questions with *Have you ever*, the past participles of the verbs in brackets and your own ideas.

0 *Have you ever been to a desert?* (be)
1 _____ (fly)
2 _____ (eat)
3 _____ (swim)
4 _____ (ride)
5 _____ (break)

READING

1 Read the emails quickly. Who do you think is going to have the most exciting weekend, Julia or Marta?

✓ PREPARE FOR THE EXAM

Reading Part 5

2 For each question, write the correct answer. Write **one** word for each gap.

To: Julia
From: Marta
Reply Forward ✉

Hi Julia,

Thanks for your invitation to go camping **(0)** _____with_____ you at Green River this weekend. I'm afraid I can't because I **(1)** _____ going skiing this Saturday for the first time. **(2)** _____ you ever tried it? I think it will **(3)** _____ good fun.

Marta

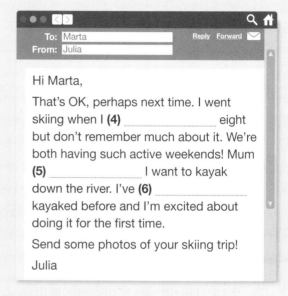

To: Marta
From: Julia
Reply Forward ✉

Hi Marta,

That's OK, perhaps next time. I went skiing when I **(4)** _____ eight but don't remember much about it. We're both having such active weekends! Mum **(5)** _____ I want to kayak down the river. I've **(6)** _____ kayaked before and I'm excited about doing it for the first time.

Send some photos of your skiing trip!

Julia

✓ **EXAM TIPS**

- Look at the word before and after each space.
- Think about what kind of word goes in each space.

3 Read the adverts below for the places from the emails in Exercise 2. Then write *A*, *B* or *A and B* for each sentence.

1 Marta is going there this weekend. ....
2 Julia is going there this weekend. ....
3 Some classes for adults cost more than for children. ....
4 You can learn to do an activity that you haven't done before. ....

5 You can rent some clothes you will need for the activity. ....
6 It is possible to book a place to stay which is at the activity centre. ....
7 You can learn an activity there in December. ....

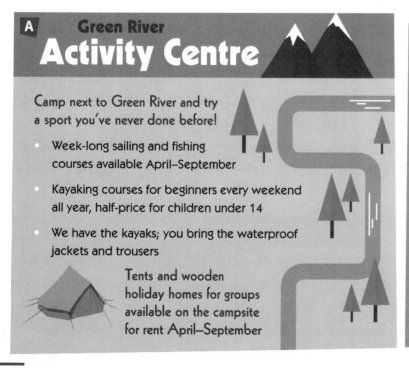

A Green River
Activity Centre

Camp next to Green River and try a sport you've never done before!

- Week-long sailing and fishing courses available April–September
- Kayaking courses for beginners every weekend all year, half-price for children under 14
- We have the kayaks; you bring the waterproof jackets and trousers

Tents and wooden holiday homes for groups available on the campsite for rent April–September

B
High Hill
Winter Activity Centre
Skiing for the first time?

> Weekend or week-long courses available November–March, staying in one of the many hotels in High Hill village (only 1 km away from the centre) – why not let us book the hotel for you?

> Special weekend offer for adult and child beginners: four lessons for the price of three

> Rent everything you need to ski from us, including jackets and boots

LISTENING

🔊 13 **1** Listen to a TV interview with a rock climber and tick (✓) the things they talk about.

A why Agnes enjoys being on TV ....
B Agnes's family ....
C other work that Agnes has done ....

D Agnes's favourite rock ....
E how Agnes feels when climbing ....

🔊 13 **2** Listen again. Are the sentences right (✓) or wrong (✗)?

1 She has been on two TV shows. ....
2 She has been scared when climbing. ....
3 She has been excited when climbing. ....
4 She has climbed with her husband. ....

5 She has been on a climbing trip with her son. ....
6 She has climbed 300 metres in one day. ....
7 She has worked in a museum. ....

WRITING — A report about a questionnaire

1 Read the article from a teenagers' magazine and answer the questions.

1 What is the name of the magazine?
....

2 When did the magazine give readers the questionnaire?
....

3 Where did readers give their answers?
....

4 How many people gave their answers?
....

5 Which school experiences have you had? Tick (✓) the *You* column in the questionnaire.
....

2 Read the questionnaire in Exercise 1 again and complete the report about questions 1–5 only.

School experiences questionnaire, questions 1–5
In last month's questionnaire about school experiences, [1] .... students gave their answers to the questions. None of the students who gave their answers have [2] .... and all of the students have [3] .... Most of the students have swum in a sports class and [4] .... Some of the students have [5] ....

3 Write a report about questions 6–10 in the questionnaire in Exercise 1.

School experiences questionnaire, questions 6–10

....
....
....
....
....
....
....
....
....
....
....
....
....
....
....
....
....
....
....
....
....
....
....
....

School experiences – *your answers!*

YOLO! Magazine wanted to know all about your school life and gave you this questionnaire last month. 6,126 of you went on our website and gave these answers to the questions.

	Have you ever ...	Yes	You (✓)
1	grown plants at school?	80%	
2	flown somewhere for a school trip?	0%	
3	swum in a sports class?	95%	
4	eaten something in a classroom?	100%	
5	ridden a bike to school?	45%	
6	broken a bone at school?	15%	
7	been excited about doing an activity at school?	100%	
8	had a great teacher at school?	83%	
9	made something useful at school?	94%	
10	looked for fossils on a school trip?	0%	

14 SPENDING MONEY

Shops

1 Match the words in the box to the pictures.

> bookshop   café   chemist   clothes shop   department store
> market   shoe shop   supermarket   sweet shop

1 _____

2 _____

3 _____

4 _____

5 _____

6 _____

7 _____

8 _____

9 _____

2 Choose the things which you <u>can't</u> usually buy in the shops.

0 bookshop	a dictionary	a notebook	(a drum)	a diary
1 bakery	bread	a cake	biscuits	a video game
2 clothes shop	a jacket	a map	jeans	a T-shirt
3 market	bananas	carrots	cameras	eggs
4 shoe shop	shoes	trainers	boots	trousers
5 supermarket	a piano	cereal	a cucumber	lemonade
6 sweet shop	chocolate	tomatoes	lollipops	sweets
7 newsagent's	jewellery	newspapers	magazines	comics
8 butcher's	burgers	meat	chicken legs	grapes

GRAMMAR — Present perfect with *just, yet* and *already*

1 Choose the correct words to complete the sentences.

1 Have you bought anything from the new clothes shop *yet / just*?
2 Sasha has *already / just* missed the train. It left only a minute ago.
3 The new supermarket has *already / yet* opened. I went there last week.
4 I've *yet / just* seen Jon. He was in his favourite place: the sweet shop.
5 I haven't been to the market *yet / already*. Do you need anything?
6 I've *just / already* seen that film three times. I love it!

2 Complete the conversation with *yet* and *already*.

Nicola: You look busy, Alex.

Alex: I am. I haven't finished my history project ¹_____.

Nicola: That's OK. We don't have to give it to Mr Cameron until Monday.

Alex: Have you finished yours ²_____?

Nicola: Yes, I've ³_____ done mine.

Alex: That's good. I've had three projects to do this week.

Nicola: Have you done your geography project ⁴_____?

Alex: Yes, I have. I did that this morning.

Nicola: Good. Why don't you come with me for a coffee? I haven't had a break ⁵_____ this morning.

Alex: I've ⁶_____ had a break.

Nicola: Have another one – you look tired.

3 What's just happened? Write complete sentences.

0 I / eat / sandwich
I've just eaten a sandwich.

1 She / play / tennis match

2 He / get home

3 We / see / concert

4 They / leave / shoe shop

4 Correct the mistakes in three of the sentences. Which two are correct?

1 I've just had a birthday, and my friend Ava bought me a CD.

2 Yesterday, I left a book at your house and I need it because I don't do my homework yet.

3 I'm just watched the football game with my family. It was really fun.

4 I'm going to paint my bedroom next week, and you've already said that you're going to help me.

5 I'm in England. I haven't seen much already because it's rained every day.

1 Match the letters and symbols to the words.

1	cm _____	**a**	cents
2	kg _____	**b**	litres
3	€ _____	**c**	pence
4	c _____	**d**	euros
5	ml _____	**e**	grams
6	m _____	**f**	millilitres
7	£ _____	**g**	kilometres
8	p _____	**h**	centimetres
9	l _____	**i**	kilograms
10	g _____	**j**	dollars
11	km _____	**k**	pounds
12	$ _____	**l**	metres

2 Complete the sentences with a word, letters or a symbol in Exercise 1.

1 There are 1,000 _____ in a litre.

2 In the UK, a Big Mac burger costs about _____ 3.20.

3 People use _____ to buy things in Spain.

4 There are 1,000 metres in a _____.

5 In one dollar, there are 100 _____.

3 Complete the text with the words in the box.

pair	set	slices	variety

Today I went to the shopping centre and spent seven months' pocket money! I bought a ¹_____ of trainers, some pens in a ²_____ of different colours and a ³_____ of Robert Pattinson DVDs. I also bought a chocolate cake, and when I got home, I ate two ⁴_____ of it while I watched my new DVDs.

1 Read the text and choose the correct answer.
What does this article do?

A It explains why people should not go shopping.
B It gives readers advice about how to stop spending money.
C It tells young people how to get more money to spend.

SPENDING MONEY

Different people do different things with money when they have it. Some keep it until they can buy something they really want, and some spend it all very quickly.

Do you spend too much money? Do you spend your money as soon as you get it? Lots of teenagers love shopping, and ¹ _____ . But if you want to keep your money for longer, read our tips.

- In a notebook, write down ² _____ . Look at your list at the end of the month and decide if anything was not a good thing to buy.

- When you go shopping, take a list of all the things you want to buy and ³ _____ .

- Buy things from a market. The prices are often better there ⁴ _____ .

- When you are in a shop, ask yourself: why am I buying this – ⁵ _____ or do I only want it at this minute?

- Don't buy something *only* because it's cheaper than usual. You probably don't really need it.

- Use cash if possible – ⁶ _____ it is too easy to forget how much you are spending. You can't spend more cash than you've got!

- Do things that are fun and free: talk to friends, go for a walk, ride your bike, play board games or ⁷ _____ .

2 There are seven phrases and sentences missing. Choose the correct place in the article for A–G.

A than in shops
B try not to buy anything else
C it is a favourite free-time activity for lots of people
D will I really want it or need to use it tomorrow

E when you use a bank card
F borrow a book from the library
G everything that you buy each month

LISTENING

🔊 **1** Listen to Marie and Harry talking about a shopping
14   trip. Tick (✓) the things you hear in the conversation.

A a plan for Saturday _____
B directions to a sports shop _____
C information about things they
   have both bought _____
D a price _____
E an invitation _____
F a phone number _____
G a shopping list _____

🔊 **2** Listen again and write one or two words or
14   a number for each answer.

1 Harry bought a pair of _____ .
2 Harry bought them in a _____ .
3 Harry spent _____ euros.
4 Harry's money was from his _____ .
5 Marie goes to football matches every
   _____ .
6 Marie goes to football matches with her
   _____ .
7 Harry has _____ watched a
   football match with Marie.

WRITING — An email

1 Rewrite the sentences with the correct punctuation.

0 I've just seen nicola.
I've just seen Nicola.

1 What time shall we meet

2 Lets go home.

3 I need to buy something from the market

4 I saw mr Smith yesterday.

2 Rewrite the emails with capital letters, apostrophes, full stops, commas and question marks.

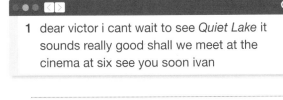

1 dear victor i cant wait to see *Quiet Lake* it sounds really good shall we meet at the cinema at six see you soon ivan

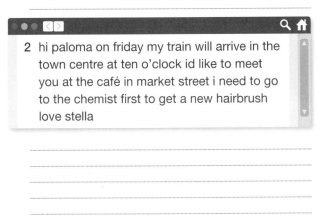

2 hi paloma on friday my train will arrive in the town centre at ten o'clock id like to meet you at the café in market street i need to go to the chemist first to get a new hairbrush love stella

3 Read email 2 from Stella again and complete the notes.

0 who the email is to: _____*Paloma*_____
1 what time her train will arrive in the town centre:

2 where to meet: _____
3 what she needs to do in town: _____

PREPARE FOR THE EXAM

Writing Part 6

4 You are going to meet your friend Kim at the shopping centre on Saturday. Write an email to Kim.

Say:
- **what time** your bus will arrive at the shopping centre
- **where** to meet
- **what** you want to do at the shopping centre.

Write **25 words** or more.

EXAM TIPS

- Include information about the three ideas in the question.
- Use informal English because you are writing to a friend.

15 FREE TIME

VOCABULARY Free-time activities

1 Match the activity to the phrase that describes it.

1 going shopping .... a having conversations
2 acting .... b using a camera
3 chatting .... c buying things
4 photography .... d being someone in a drama
5 cooking .... e making music with a guitar or violin, for example
6 playing an instrument .... f having a game of tennis, for example
7 collecting things .... g moving your body, usually to music
8 dancing .... h getting and keeping lots of one kind of object
9 playing sport .... i making things to eat

2 Read about the people's hobbies and complete the texts with the words in the box.

| acting   chatting   collecting   cooking   going (x2)   listening   making |
| photography   playing (x2)   reading   singing   spending   watching |

I really like [1] .... time online and [2] .... to other people on my phone and laptop. I also love [3] .... to music online. I live on the internet!

Galina

I love [8] .... computer games and [9] .... TV. I like [10] .... books too. I go to the library every week.

Pilar

My favourite hobby is [4] .... things from plastic, wood and paper. I'm learning [5] .... too, so I usually take pictures of them when I've finished them.

Tanya

In my free time I enjoy [11] .... musical instruments. I'm quite good at the piano and the drums. I also like [12] .... instruments – I've got about 30 different ones already!

Nala

[6] .... is my favourite thing to do when I'm not in school. I love [7] .... shopping for food that I haven't used before, then making something amazing with it.

Guillermo

I go to a theatre group every Saturday morning and we do three things which I love: [13] .... in plays, [14] .... songs and dancing. I like [15] .... out with my friends from the group too – they're great fun.

Lev

GRAMMAR Present perfect with *for* and *since*

1 Choose the correct words to complete the sentences.

1 I've had my phone *for* / *since* six months.
2 She's had her computer *for* / *since* 2013.
3 They've lived there *for* / *since* last summer.
4 He's only played the guitar *for* / *since* three weeks.
5 I haven't seen my cousins *for* / *since* a long time.
6 We have known each other *for* / *since* we were ten years old.

2 Tick (✓) the correct sentences.

1 A It's so nice that you'll come tomorrow. I didn't see you for three weeks.
 B It's so nice that you'll come tomorrow. I haven't seen you for three weeks.
2 A I didn't eat chicken since a long time.
 B I haven't eaten chicken for a long time.
3 A Yesterday I bought two dresses. I haven't had one since I was six!
 B Yesterday I bought two dresses. I've never had one since I was six!
4 A I want to sell my radio. I've had it for four years.
 B I want to sell my radio. I've got it since four years.
5 A I know Adam 20 years.
 B I've known Adam for 20 years.

3 Rewrite the sentences using *for* or *since*. Imagine it is now 7 pm on Monday 21st August.

0 We've lived here since 21st June.
 We've lived here for two months.
1 I've had a headache for three hours.

2 Josh has had that camera since April.

3 Aysha and Faruk have been out with their friends since 2 pm.

4 Davina's only played the violin for a month.

5 You haven't phoned me since last Monday.

6 The rain hasn't stopped for 24 hours.

4 Complete the blog with *for*, *since*, *has* or *have*.

I collect postcards. I've collected them ¹ _____ a long time. I started when I was six and I'm thirteen now, so I've had this hobby ² _____ seven years. I started when my uncle sent me a postcard from Madrid. He ³ _____ visited a penfriend there every year ⁴ _____ he was a teenager. All my friends and family ⁵ _____ sent me postcards ⁶ _____ then. My favourite is a postcard that ⁷ _____ been on my bedroom wall ⁸ _____ I was ten. It's a photo of New Zealand.

VOCABULARY Collocations about having fun

1 Choose the correct words to complete the sentences.

1 When I go camping with my friends, I always _____ a brilliant time.
 A enjoy   B have   C spend
2 My mum's family are from Argentina and I love _____ time with them when we go there for holidays.
 A being   B feeling   C spending
3 I collect old watches, and finding an unusual one gives me a fantastic _____ .
 A time   B laugh   C feeling
4 When you do a free-time activity, the most important thing is to _____ yourself.
 A enjoy   B laugh   C play
5 Everyone was really _____ when Georgina won the photography prize – her photos were much more interesting than anyone else's.
 A great   B fun   C glad

2 Write sentences about you using the phrases in the box.

| a laugh | an exciting weekend |
| enjoy ourselves | spending time |

0 *I always have a laugh with my eldest sister!*
1
2
3
4

READING

1 Read the blog quickly. What is Sascha's hobby? Would you like to try this hobby? Why? / Why not?

MAKING SHOES

FOR FUN

A blog by **Sascha Marr, aged 14**

My hobby is making shoes. It's an unusual hobby, but I love the fantastic feeling of wearing shoes that I've made myself.

I've always liked designing things. I remember drawing clothes and shoes when I was eight, and I made my first skirt aged nine. Then three years ago, I began making shoes, and I now spend my free time doing that.

I became interested in making shoes when my cousin told me about an online shoe-making course that he was doing. I immediately wanted to do one too. Mum booked me on a four-day course at the I Can Make Shoes school in London to see if I liked it, and then I did a ten-day course there in the summer holidays.

I loved the courses. On the longer one, I made four pairs of shoes! I couldn't believe it. The teachers were excellent. That's what was best about the classes. They made us work really hard but they wanted all their students to have fun, too.

I've made about 15 pairs of shoes now. At the moment I'm making a pair of trainers using an old pair of jeans, but I've used all kinds of different things before, from old leather handbags to old cotton dresses!

Making shoes has changed my plans for the future. I know now that I want to be a designer, but not a shoe designer. I've decided I'll do home design. I've designed lots of shoes and also some clothes, so I'd like to try something new.

✓ PREPARE FOR THE EXAM

Reading Part 3

2 For each question, choose the correct answer.

1 Making shoes has been Sascha's hobby
   A for eight years.
   B since she was nine.
   C for three years.

2 The first course that Sascha did in shoe making was
   A an online course.
   B four days long.
   C ten days long.

3 What did Sascha like most about the courses?
   A having fun with the other students
   B getting lots of shoes
   C having such good teachers

4 The shoes that Sascha is working on now are made from
   A old jeans.
   B old handbags.
   C old dresses.

5 In the future, Sascha would like to be
   A a shoe designer.
   B a home designer.
   C a clothes designer.

✓ EXAM TIPS

- Before you read the text, look at the title and the photo to get an idea of what it's about.
- You should always answer all the questions. If you aren't sure what the correct answer to a question is, choose the one that you think is right.

1 Listen to Dilek and Burak and choose the best summary of what they talk about.

  A choosing a free-time activity
  B free-time activities in my country
  C my favourite free-time activity

2 Listen again. Are the sentences right (✓) or wrong (✗)?

  1 Dilek has been a dancer for ten years. ....
  2 Dilek's dance group usually meets twice every week. ....
  3 Dilek dances at weddings. ....
  4 Dilek dances to rock music. ....
  5 Dilek always wears a special dress when she dances. ....
  6 The oud is easy to play. ....
  7 Burak started playing the oud when he was six. ....
  8 Burak's dad was Burak's teacher. ....
  9 Burak can also play the guitar. ....
  10 Burak would like to be a singer when he is older. ....

WRITING A post on an online forum

1 Read the post. Then match the parts of the text A–E to the questions below.

  1 What do you do with these things now? ....
  2 How long have you collected them? ....
  3 What do you like about these things? ....
  4 What do you collect? ....
  5 Why did you start collecting them? ....

Patrick

(A) I collect comics. **(B)** I have collected them for nine years. **(C)** I started collecting them when I was six because I liked reading them. I bought them every week with my pocket money. **(D)** Now I still enjoy reading them every day, and I often look for special comics online. The oldest ones are very expensive. **(E)** I like comics because they have great stories, they're funny and the pictures are amazing. You're never too old to read a comic!

2 Imagine you have responded to the questions with the answers given. Write a post on an online forum using the notes.

  1 What do you collect? — board games
  2 How long have you collected them? — five years
  3 Why did you start collecting them? — loved playing them
  4 What do you do with these things now? — play them with best friend and brother
  5 What do you like about these things? — all so different, have fun when I play them

  I collect board games.
  ....
  ....
  ....
  ....
  ....
  ....
  ....

16 LANGUAGES OF THE WORLD

VOCABULARY | Words to describe language learning

1 Match the questions to the answers.

1 What is the **topic** of Unit 16? _____
2 Which words on this page are difficult to **spell**? _____
3 What is the **meaning** of 'mistake'? _____
4 Can you **translate** 'guess' into Spanish, please? _____
5 Where do you find lots of **articles**? _____
6 When do you make a **list**? _____
7 Where do you **look up** words you don't know? _____
8 How many **exercises** are there on this page? _____

a on a news website
b in a dictionary
c learning languages
d something that is not correct
e four
f 'exercise' and 'vocabulary'
g *adivinar*
h before going shopping

2 Read the web page about learning languages and complete the text with the words in the box.

| articles | exercises | guess | list | look it up | mistakes | spell | topics | translate |

Tips for learning languages

Home | About us | Contact us

We'd like to give you some tips for learning languages. Learning a language is one of the most useful things you can do with your free time. It's hard work, but it's also a lot of fun. These are some things you can do to help improve your level in the languages you are studying.

- Read as many books and magazine or news [1] _____ as possible.
- Listen as often as you can to the radio, to songs and to people talking about lots of different [2] _____, so your pronunciation and vocabulary improve.
- Don't worry about making [3] _____.
- Do grammar and vocabulary [4] _____ online or in workbooks.
- Learn how to [5] _____ words correctly.
- Make a [6] _____ of new vocabulary and then play games with the words to help you learn them.
- When you read or hear a word you don't know, try to [7] _____ its meaning. You can then [8] _____ in a dictionary. But remember that it is sometimes not possible to [9] _____ a word from one language to another exactly.

hola
привет
merhaba
olá ciao
你好
cześć
hello

GRAMMAR | Present perfect and past simple

1 Choose the correct verbs to complete the sentences.

1 *Did / Have* you ever studied Arabic?
2 *Did / Have* you do any tests in school last week?
3 *Did / Has* anyone in your family learned to speak four languages?
4 When *did / have* you first study English?
5 How long *did / have* you been an English student?

2 Answer the questions in Exercise 1 for you.

1 _____
2 _____
3 _____
4 _____
5 _____

3 Write sentences in the present perfect or past simple.

0 she / work / in New Zealand and South Africa
She's worked in New Zealand and South Africa.

1 I / never / meet / anyone / from the USA

2 we / go / to Cyprus / last year

3 he / study / Chinese and Arabic / two years ago

4 she / watch / a great cricket match / on Saturday

5 he / not win / any chess competitions / since 2009

6 we / not see / my grandparents / last month

7 I / never / eat / Mexican food

4 <u>Underline</u> seven mistakes with the present perfect and past simple in the email.

Hi David,

It's been ages since I haven't heard from you! I'm in London now. I'm studying at the Camden School of English! I met lots of people from all over the world here. The teacher is good and the textbook she gave us at the beginning of the course is very interesting. I learn a lot of things from it since then.

Every day, after class, we go into the centre of London. I've already done lots of things! I've the British Museum. It was great! I've went shopping in a market yesterday and bought some clothes. I've bought three T-shirts in the market because they were very cheap and they look really nice. They have only cost me £20.

Right, I must go now. I've got to study for an English test tomorrow – it's on the present perfect.

Love,

Danuta

5 Correct the mistakes in Exercise 4.

1
2
3
4
5
6
7

1 Match the numbers to the words.

1 two billion
2 twenty thousand eight hundred and twenty
3 two hundred million
4 two hundred and twenty-five

a 200,000,000
b 225
c 2,000,000,000
d 20,820

2 Read the text and answer the questions. Write numbers for your answers.

ONE WORLD, MANY LANGUAGES

There are about seven billion people in the world today and there are about seven thousand, one hundred languages. But about four billion people speak just twenty-three of these languages as their first language. More than fifty million people speak each of these languages.

0 How many people live in the word today?
about *7,000,000,000*

1 How many languages are there in the world today?
about

2 How many people speak just 23 of the world's languages?
about

3 How many people speak each of the 23 languages?
over

3 Answer the questions with words. Go online to find the answers.

0 How many people live in the UK?
Sixty-five million people live in the UK.

1 How many people live in your country?

2 How many people in the world speak your first language?

3 How many languages are there in your country?

1 Read the article. Then choose the paragraph(s) where you find the information 1–4.

1 the number of people living in China and Japan	Paragraph 1 2 3
2 the first languages of China and Japan	Paragraph 1 2 3
3 the size of China and Japan	Paragraph 1 2 3
4 the world's four largest countries	Paragraph 1 2 3

SOME DIFFERENCES BETWEEN
CHINA AND JAPAN

1 China is a very large country in East Asia, with grass lands, deserts, mountains, lakes, rivers and more than 14,000 kilometres of coast. China covers an area of 9,388,211 square kilometres. Only Russia, Canada and the USA are larger. China has about 300 languages that people in different parts of the country speak as a first language. About 848,000,000 Chinese people speak Mandarin, more than any of the other Chinese languages. This is also a lot more than the total number of people who speak both English and Spanish as a first language. More people speak Mandarin in China's cities than in the countryside.

2 Japan is also in East Asia. It is a group of 6,852 islands, some very large and some very small. Tokyo, the capital, is on the island of Honshu. The area that Japan covers is much smaller than China. Sixty-two other countries in the world are larger than Japan, including Norway, Mali and Mexico. It has 364,555 square kilometres of land. Most people in Japan speak Japanese as their first language. It has six or seven other languages, but very few people speak these.

3 1,409,517,397 people live in China, and 127,484,450 people live in Japan. This means that for every square kilometre of China, there are 150 people. But in Japan, there are 350 people for every square kilometre. There are only nine countries in the world with more people than Japan, including China – China has more people living in it than any other country.

2 Read the text again and match the sentence halves.

1 Fourteen thousand kilometres is the length of the	**a** Mandarin.
2 China is smaller than	**b** nearly all Japanese people.
3 Most Chinese speakers' first language is	**c** three other countries.
4 There are six thousand eight hundred and fifty-two	**d** people for every square kilometre of Japan.
5 Japan is the sixty-third	**e** largest country in the world.
6 There are three hundred and fifty	**f** islands in Japan.
7 Japanese is the first language of	**g** Chinese coast.

PREPARE FOR THE EXAM

Listening Part 4

1 For each question, choose the correct answer.

🔊 **1** You will hear a girl called Lucy talking to her
16   mum. What are they discussing?
   A when Lucy will eat this evening
   B how Lucy will get to basketball practice
   C if Lucy's mum can work late

2 You will hear a girl called Sam talking to her
friend about playing musical instruments. Why
does she prefer the piano to the guitar?
   A She plays a variety of music on the piano.
   B Too many other people play the guitar.
   C The guitar is more difficult.

3 You will hear a girl talking about her Chinese
homework. What is she explaining?
   A She needs the most time to do the listening
   exercise.
   B She enjoys doing the writing exercises.
   C She has only done the reading exercise
   today.

4 You will hear a boy talking about his English
lesson today. What does he say about it?
   A He used his dictionary a lot.
   B His teacher could not help him.
   C The work he had to do was hard.

5 You will hear a girl called Sophie talking to a
friend about an article she read. What was the
topic of the article?
   A how to learn lots of languages
   B why it is good to learn languages
   C the best age to learn more languages

 EXAM TIPS

- You will hear each conversation twice like this:
Conversation 1, Conversation 1, Conversation 2,
Conversation 2, etc.
- Check your answer the second time you listen.

WRITING   A text about languages and you

1 Read the text and correct it with capital letters.

> C
> My name is ᴄarys and I am from wales, which
>
> is a country in the uk (the united kingdom of
>
> great britain and northern ireland). the uk is
>
> in europe. wales has two languages: welsh
>
> and english. most people in wales speak
>
> english, but many also speak welsh. At home
>
> I speak english because my parents are from
>
> scotland. I learn welsh at school. I also learn
>
> spanish and french at school.

2 Write notes about you. Don't forget to use
capital letters.

Your name: _____
Your country and its continent: _____
Languages of your country: _____
Language(s) you speak at home: _____
Language(s) you learn at school / another place:
_____

3 Write a paragraph using your notes from
Exercise 2. Write 50–70 words.

_____
_____
_____
_____
_____
_____
_____
_____
_____
_____
_____
_____
_____
_____
_____

17 STAYING HEALTHY

VOCABULARY   Body parts

1 Put the letters in the correct order to make body parts.

1 o d o b l ....
2 k a b c ....
3 r n a b i ....
4 a t h r e ....
5 n u t o e g ....

6 t m b u h ....
7 g i r e n f ....
8 l a k n e ....
9 c e n k ....
10 t o a c s h m ....

2 Circle the word which <u>doesn't</u> belong in each column.

1 This is inside your body.	2 This is below your head.	3 This has bones in it.	4 This is above your back.	5 You can make this move.	6 This is smaller than a brain.
heart	neck	finger	neck	toe	back
ear	toe	back	heart	finger	toe
blood	brain	toe	brain	brain	ear
stomach	back	ankle	ear	neck	heart
		stomach		tongue	thumb

3 Complete the sentences with the words in the box.

ankle	back	blood	brains	ears	fingers	heart	neck	stomach	toes

1 People and animals have two .... We hear with them.
2 You point with one of the .... on your hand.
3 .... is red and you see it if something cuts you.
4 You get hungry when your .... is empty.
5 People are cleverer than many other animals because their .... are quite large.
6 A giraffe has a very long ....
7 A horse can carry a person on its ....
8 Your .... are at the end of your feet.
9 The .... is usually on the left side of your body, and it has to work harder when you do exercise.
10 Your .... is between your foot and your knee.

GRAMMAR   Reflexive pronouns *myself, yourself, herself, himself, itself, ourselves, yourselves, themselves*

1 Match 1–8 to a–h.

1 I ....
2 you (singular) ....
3 he ....
4 she ....
5 it ....
6 we ....
7 you (plural) ....
8 they ....

a themselves
b himself
c ourselves
d myself
e yourselves
f herself
g yourself
h itself

2 Choose the correct words to complete the sentences.

1 He's teaching *himself / yourselves* to speak Arabic.
2 Did you paint that wall by *yourself / themselves*?
3 We really enjoyed *yourselves / ourselves* on holiday.
4 They bought *himself / themselves* a new video game.
5 She made the cake by *itself / herself*.
6 I hurt *yourself / myself* playing football.

3 **Complete the sentences with the correct reflexive pronouns.**

1 Cindi hurt ………………………… when she fell off her bike.
2 My dad always says to me, 'Look after …………………………!' when I leave the house.
3 'Help ………………………… to chocolate cake,' my aunt told us when we got to her house.
4 He hasn't made a meal by ………………………… before. I hope he uses a cookbook!
5 We really enjoyed ………………………… at Dan's birthday party.
6 Sometimes I like to go to the cinema by ………………………… .
7 My brothers taught ………………………… to play tennis and are now quite good players.
8 There is a beautiful tree in the park. It stands by ………………………… near the river.

4 **Correct the mistakes in three of the sentences. Which two are correct?**

1 He hurt himself playing cricket.
…………………………………………………………
2 Yesterday I went to buy me some clothes.
…………………………………………………………
3 I'm so happy that I'm coming to your house tomorrow. We'll enjoy us.
…………………………………………………………
…………………………………………………………
4 You take care of your self.
…………………………………………………………
5 She bought herself a new laptop.
…………………………………………………………

VOCABULARY Adjectives to express emotion

1 **Use the clues below to complete the crossword.**

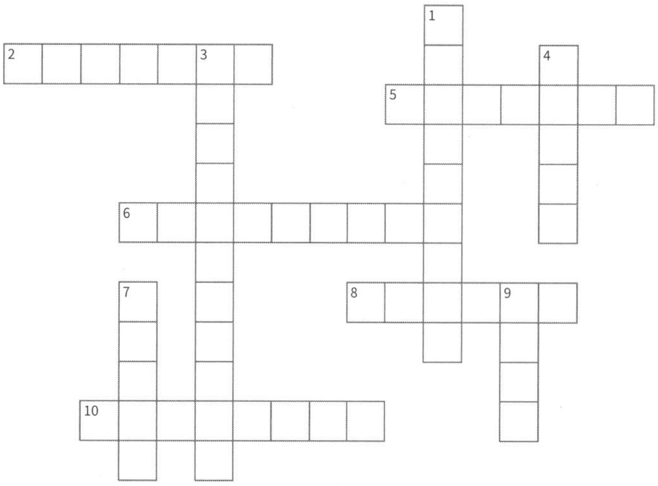

Across

2 Nick is ………………………… about his new school because he doesn't have any friends there.
5 Freddie never looks ………………………… – he's always laughing.
6 Henry was ………………………… to see Lena at the party – he thought she was on holiday.
8 Mark was the only person at home yesterday evening. He felt ………………………… and was glad when his parents came home.
10 The people I met at Art Club were very nice. They were all really ………………………… to me.

Down

1 Jane is very ………………………… – she never feels shy.
3 Maddy was in a café when she dropped a cup and broke it. She felt really ………………………… when everyone in the café turned and looked at her.
4 When you feel ………………………… about something, it's good to talk to someone about it.
7 The students were ………………………… because the canteen was closed and they were hungry.
9 Jenna is not a ………………………… person. She's very active.

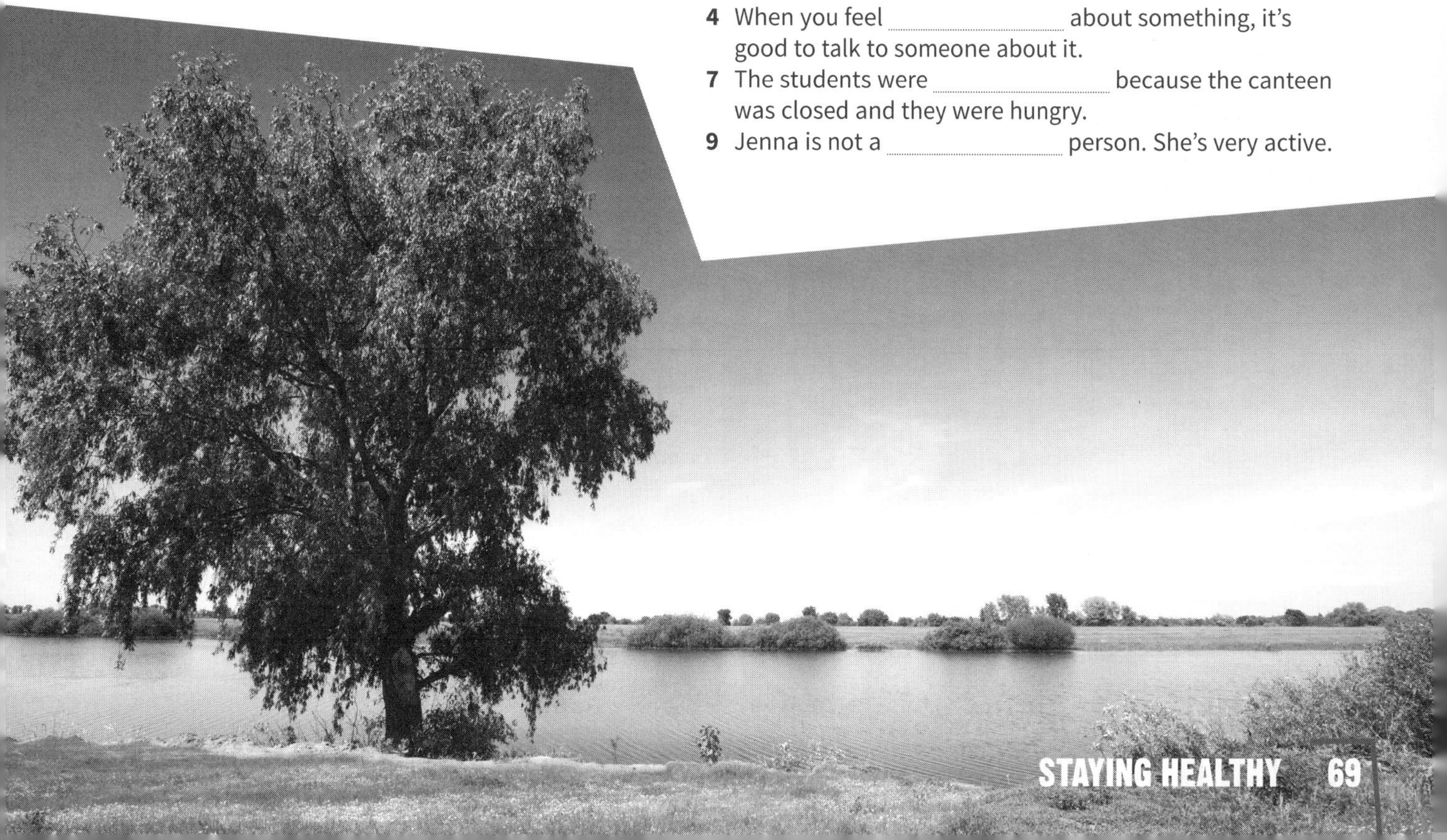

1 Read the article and complete the text with the words and phrases in the box. There is one extra word or phrase.

| family | friends | money | schoolwork |
| sport | staying healthy | | |

What's most important to you?

Five teenagers talk about the things that are most important to them.

Olga

At the moment I'm worried about my ¹ _____. It's really important to me. I'm only 14, but I already know what I want to do when I'm older: I want to be a heart doctor. That means I can never be lazy, and I must do well in every exam.

Sergey

The most important thing for me is ² _____. We should all look after ourselves. I do yoga every day and it makes my whole body feel great. It's very good for my neck and back, which sometimes hurt when I've sat at a desk all day.

Michael

I don't have any brothers or sisters but I'm never lonely because of my ³ _____. I don't think anything is more important to me than them. We do everything together – go to the cinema, do sports, chat and study at home.

Isabella

It's easy to say what's important to me: ⁴ _____ ! I love doing all kinds of it. I'm in three school teams so I practise six days a week. Sunday is the one day when I can be lazy, and I watch matches and tournaments on TV then.

Paulina

My ⁵ _____ are more important to me than anything. We spend a lot of time together and help each other when we're unhappy. We always eat our evening meal together. My cousins often come to dinner, too, and then there are 15 of us around the table. We have a great time.

2 Read the text again. Are the sentences right (✓) or wrong (✗)?

1 Olga has already decided about her future job. ....
2 Sergey only does yoga at the weekend. ....
3 Michael's family are more important than his friends. ....
4 Isabella enjoys being active. ....
5 Paulina enjoys eating with lots of other people. ....

PREPARE FOR THE EXAM

Listening Part 1

1 For each question, choose the correct picture.

🔊 17 **1** How much did Monica pay for her keyboard?

A £90 **B** £120 **C** £450

2 What time will the football match finish?

A **B** **C**

3 When is the history test?

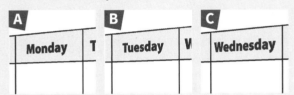

A		B		C	
Monday	T	Tuesday	V	Wednesday	

4 Where is the girl's purse?

A   **B**   **C**

5 What is the girl's father doing now?

A   **B**   **C**

EXAM TIPS

- Before you listen, think in English about what each picture shows.
- <u>Underline</u> the most important words in the question.

WRITING — Giving advice on a forum

1 Read the student's problem on an online forum. Are the sentences below right (✓) or wrong (✗)?

When I have an exam at school, I get very worried in the week before I have to do it. I study really hard for the exam every day, but I think about all the things that might go wrong and then I don't sleep very well. This means that on the day of the exam, I usually feel very tired, and I am scared that I will forget everything I know. Can anybody give me some advice?

1 He is worried all the time at school.
2 He is lazy.
3 He finds it difficult to sleep before an exam.
4 He worries about sleeping too much.
5 He would like some advice.

2 Read the responses to the forum post in Exercise 1. Decide if the advice is good or bad.

A You shouldn't spend all your time studying. You should take lots of breaks.

B You should study more. Then you won't forget anything and you won't worry.

C How about doing some exercise? This will help you sleep at night. And why don't you study with your friends? It's more fun and they can help you feel more confident.

3 Write a response to the forum post in Exercise 1. Include three pieces of advice. Write 30–50 words.

18 FROM COVER TO COVER

VOCABULARY   Books and reading

1 Choose the correct phrases to complete the sentences.

1 When you drop something, you *pick it up* / *take it back*.

2 When you want to learn about something, you *take out* / *find out* about it.

3 When you're unhappy with something you've bought, you *put it back* / *take it back*.

4 When you go to another country, you might *bring back* / *give back* presents for your family.

5 When you are in a café, waiters *put the food down* / *take the food out* on your table.

2 Complete the sentences with a word from each box. You can use some words more than once.

bring	find	give		back	down
pick	put	take		out	up

0 That's too heavy for you to carry.
Put it down!

1 Which book are you going to .... of the library today?

2 When the teacher's ruler fell off his desk onto the floor, he asked Mark to .... it .... and .... it .... on his desk.

3 Georgia is too ill to go to her grandma's party. Her brothers are going and they will .... Georgia .... a big slice of birthday cake.

4 Mum bought me a book I've already read so I'm going to .... it .... to the book shop.

5 Thanks for lending me this jacket. I'll .... it .... to you tomorrow.

6 I don't know what time the train arrives, but I'll .... and tell you.

GRAMMAR   First conditional

1 Complete the sentences with the correct form of the verbs in brackets.

1 What will we do if it .... (rain) tomorrow?

2 I won't listen to this music if you .... (not like) it.

3 They'll be really excited if we .... (get) them tickets to the concert.

4 If Alice .... (work) hard, she'll do well in her exams.

5 I .... (be) really happy if I pass my exams.

6 If Maria doesn't go now, she .... (not see) the beginning of the play.

7 If you do some exercise, you .... (feel) better.

8 If it's hot and sunny at the weekend, we .... (go) swimming with my friends.

9 If you .... (eat) more fruit and vegetables, you'll be healthier.

2 Write sentences in the first conditional.

1 If / I not finish my project / I not come to / the cinema with you

2 We / get fitter / if / we do more exercise / each week

3 She / learn Portuguese / if / she move to Brazil

4 They / be late for the dentist / if / they not leave now

5 If / we not win / the match on Saturday / we be very upset

6 If / he work hard / he pass his Russian exam

3 Correct the mistakes in the sentences.

1 If you come too, you love it.

2 I think it be OK if we meet at the park at ten o'clock in the morning.

3 I will bring some banana pancake for you if my mum made it for me.

4 If you don't have any, I give you some.

5 If you can visit Vietnam, I'll took you to Vũng Tàu and lots of beautiful places.

VOCABULARY — Words about books

1 Match the questions to the answers.

1 Where do people often keep their books?
2 What can you do with some paper and some crayons or pencils?
3 What is on this **page**?
4 What question asks for someone's **opinion**?
5 What is the **title** of this unit?
6 What are the sections in a story called?
7 What is the opposite of 'the beginning'?
8 What is the stronger, outside part of a book called?
9 What word means someone who writes books?

a some English exercises
b the **cover**
c on a **shelf**
d the **end**
e 'From cover to cover'
f **author**
g What do you think?
h a **drawing**
i **chapters**

2 Read the notices and messages. <u>Underline</u> four phrasal verbs from Vocabulary Exercise 2 on page 72.

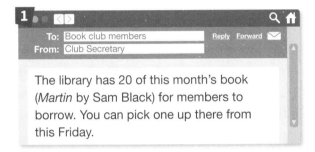

1
To: Book club members   Reply Forward
From: Club Secretary

The library has 20 of this month's book (*Martin* by Sam Black) for members to borrow. You can pick one up there from this Friday.

2
Katie, I'm taking a book back to the bookshop today. Can I get you anything while I'm there? Mum

3
Don't take dictionaries out of the library. Use them in the study area.

4

Sarah, 14.50

I agree with the last person's post. This book's great, especially the last few pages. I couldn't put it down.

5
Competition!

Design a cover for your favourite story book!
Prizes for the best three!

6
Isabel, I've just seen an advertisement for a talk by author Sammy Coles. It's at the bookshop tonight. I can go, can you? Elena

✓ PREPARE FOR THE EXAM

Reading Part 1

3 For each question, choose the correct answer.

1 What information does this message give book club members?
   A when this month's meeting will be
   B how many books will be available
   C where the club usually meets

2 What is Katie's mum doing in this message?
   A inviting Katie to join her
   B offering to buy something for Katie
   C asking Katie to do something for her

3 What does this notice mean?
   A You cannot borrow dictionaries to read at home.
   B You must not forget to bring dictionaries back to the library.
   C You should not leave dictionaries in the study area.

4 What does Sarah say about the book?
   A She didn't finish the book.
   B She had a different opinion to someone else.
   C She thought the end was the best part.

5 For this competition, you have to
   A write something.
   B do some art.
   C make a book.

6 What does Elena want to do?
   A get information about a writer from Isabel
   B read a book she saw in a shop
   C go and listen to someone

✓ EXAM TIPS

- Read each text and think about who wrote it, and who it is for.
- The correct answer has the same meaning as the text, but it usually uses different words.

READING

1 Read the texts quickly. What kind of books do the boys read?

Uri _____

Ned _____

Mike _____

What do you read?

Three students tell us about what they read

Uri

I read a lot but it's not story books that I read. I'm a mountain climber at weekends, and I read two or three magazines a month about my sport. There are some great books about it, too – I'd like to write one myself in the future. It's only since I've been a climber that I've started reading in my free time. Before that, I didn't enjoy it much. I sometimes go on climbing websites, but I don't like reading a lot of text on a screen.

Ned

I read school textbooks but I've never picked up a book to read for fun. My parents gave me lots of books to read when I was young but I wasn't really interested. Perhaps I will be when I'm older, but at the moment, I spend a lot of time reading online. I can't take my phone to school, but I look at the news at least once a day on my phone, and I like reading about what my friends are doing.

Mike

I've always read a lot, ever since I was a young boy, and I always will. I read all kinds of things, from comics to science magazines. I also download a lot of funny ebooks and keep them on my tablet, which I take everywhere. It's great having hundreds of books on that because then, when I'm waiting for a bus or I'm bored at lunchtime, I can read one. I read things online too, but that's usually finding information for homework.

✓ PREPARE FOR THE EXAM

Reading Part 2

2 For each question, choose the correct answer. Write *U* for Uri, *N* for Ned or *M* for Mike.

1 Which person is happy to read books on a screen? _____

2 Which person thinks he might enjoy reading books more later in his life? _____

3 Which person prefers reading real books to reading digital books? _____

4 Which person reads a large variety of different things? _____

5 Which person doesn't read books in his free time? _____

6 Which person says he likes to have something to read with him all the time? _____

7 Which person reads more now than in the past? _____

✓ EXAM TIPS

- You must only choose one answer for each question.
- Don't think an answer is right just because you see the same word in the text and the question.

LISTENING

🔊 18 **1** Listen to a conversation about books and choose the correct answers.

1 Where is the conversation happening?
A in a library   **B** in a bookshop

2 Which person is having this conversation at work?
A the man   **B** the girl

🔊 18 **2** Listen again and write one word or number for each answer.

1 The girl and her _____ are going to South Africa.

2 The travel book shelves are next to the _____.

3 Today, one book will be cheaper if you get _____ books.

4 The girl doesn't know the _____ of the book for her sister.

5 The girl will find *Pictures for Life* on the _____ floor.

6 There is bigger bookshop on _____ Street.

1 Look at the pictures and read the sentences. Which picture is each sentence about? Write *1*, *2* or *3*.

0 Both boys were happy.   *3*
1 Then his little brother started playing a keyboard.
2 His younger brother was hitting a drum.
3 The music was terrible!
4 A boy was sitting on the sofa, trying to read a book.
5 The boy read a book to his little brother. The little brother was quiet.
6 The boy stopped reading and put his book down on the sofa.
7 The noise the drum made was very loud.

2 Use the sentences in Exercise 1 to complete the story. Link the sentences using *so*, *unfortunately*, *and* or *but.* More than one answer is possible.

A boy was sitting on the sofa, trying to read a book. **Unfortunately,** *his younger brother was hitting a drum* **and** *the noise the drum made was very loud.*

_____

_____

_____

_____

_____

_____

✓ **PREPARE FOR THE EXAM**

Writing Part 7

3 Look at the three pictures. Write the story shown in the pictures. Write **35 words** or more.

✓ **EXAM TIPS**
- You must write about all three pictures in your story.
- Write your story in the same order as the three pictures.

_____

_____

_____

_____

_____

_____

_____

19 DIFFERENT INGREDIENTS

VOCABULARY — Words to describe cooking

1 Find eight verbs to describe cooking.

p	r	e	p	a	r	e
h	t	s	f	d	q	c
a	l	n	k	d	u	o
d	b	o	l	l	p	v
r	g	e	v	x	m	e
y	b	a	k	e	i	r
f	i	l	l	m	x	b

2 Complete the sentences with the correct form of the verbs in Exercise 1.

1 If you put fruit like grapes out in the sun, it will .... and then you can keep it for longer.
2 You have to .... water to make tea.
3 .... the bowl with a plate and then put it in the fridge, please.
4 My brother has .... my mother a cake for her birthday.
5 You need to .... all the ingredients together in a large bowl.
6 Have you .... any salt or pepper to this soup yet?
7 I've .... some sandwiches and salad for us. Are you ready for lunch now?
8 Could you .... the bowl with water, please?

GRAMMAR — Present simple passive

1 Match the sentence halves.

1 Tea is drunk ....
2 Italian wine is ....
3 Beans are grown in ....
4 Lots of chocolate ....
5 Soup is often ....

a is produced in Belgium.
b eaten cold in Spain.
c without milk in my country.
d sold all over the world.
e Mexico.

2 Put the words in the correct order to make sentences.

1 often grown / tomatoes / are / inside
2 made / fruit / from / is / jam
3 are / with / chocolate / my favourite / biscuits / covered
4 a very hot oven / put / the cakes / are / into
5 filled / the pasta / is / cheese and mushrooms / with

3 Rewrite the sentences in the present simple passive.

0 Bakers use wheat flour to make bread.
Wheat flour is used by bakers to make bread.
1 People in most parts of the world drink tea.
2 Many children eat too much sugar.
3 Farmers in warm countries grow pineapples.
4 People in different countries make bread in different ways.
5 Some people drink coffee with ice.

4 Correct the mistakes in four of the sentences. Which one is correct?

1 The art lesson is started at ten o'clock.
2 You start off from your house, turn left, go straight on, take the second right and you are arrived there.
3 Coffee is drunk all over the world.
4 You can get the number 12 bus. It is stopped near my house.
5 The class lasts two hours and we are spent the time painting.

1 Choose the correct words to complete the sentences.

1 Green beans are a *fruit / vegetable*.
2 Melons are a large, *square / round* fruit.
3 Steak is a kind of *vegetable / meat*.
4 Pears are *white / red* inside.
5 Garlic is often eaten with *meat / ice cream*.
6 Carrots are *green / orange*.
7 *Chips / Sweets* are made with potatoes.
8 Salt and pepper are usually added to *soup / cereals*.

2 Tick (✓) the correct box(es).

	Cooked in water	Cooked inside the cooker	Cooked on top of the cooker	Cooked in some oil or butter
a fried fish				
a baked potato				
a roast chicken				
a grilled burger				
a boiled egg				

3 Choose the correct verbs to complete the phrases.

1 *make / do* a cake
2 *make / do* the cleaning
3 *make / do* a cup of tea
4 *make / do* the dishes
5 *make / do* your homework
6 *make / do* a mess
7 *make / do* a mistake
8 *make / do* the shopping
9 *make / do* the washing
10 *make / do* the bed

4 Complete the sentences with the correct form of *make* or *do*.

1 The machine broke when I was _____ the washing yesterday.
2 When I visit my grandmother, the first thing she says to me is: 'Would you like me to _____ you a cup of tea?'
3 My baby brother _____ a mess when he eats.
4 My parents always _____ the cleaning at the weekend.
5 My sister _____ me a beautiful cake for my birthday last week.
6 Have you _____ your bed today?
7 My friends think I'm crazy, but I enjoy _____ my homework.
8 Do you ever _____ the dishes at home?
9 I've _____ the shopping lots of times, but I don't enjoy it.
10 I usually _____ a lot of mistakes when I speak another language.

5 What do you do at home? What don't you do? Write sentences with *make* and *do* phrases in Exercise 3 and the words in the box.

always	never	often	sometimes	usually

1 _____
2 _____
3 _____
4 _____
5 _____

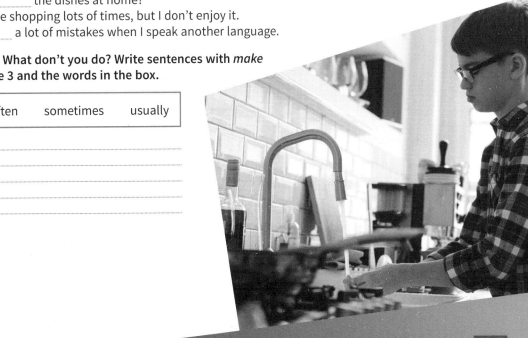

1 Read the blog quickly. What is it about?

....

 PREPARE FOR THE EXAM

Reading Part 5

2 For each question, write the correct answer. Write **one** word for each gap.

Hi, I'm Lucy. Thank you **(0)** _____ *for* visiting my blog about family life. Today, I **(1)** _____ going to tell you about our kitchen. It is **(2)** _____ most important room in this flat, which I share **(3)** _____ my mum, dad, and brother. We all love cooking so we spend lots **(4)** _____ time in this room. My brother **(5)** _____ I always make a mess when we cook, but my parents don't mind if we tidy up after we've eaten. **(6)** _____ is a large, round table in the middle of the room, and we all sit together around it each evening, chatting while we slowly eat our dinner.

 EXAM TIPS

- The second time you read something, you will see things you didn't see the first time. Don't forget to read the text more than once!
- Look at the photo and think about the topic before you read the text.

3 Read the blog. There are four sentences missing. Choose the correct place in the text for sentences A–E. There is one extra sentence that you don't need.

Blog

Hi! It's Lucy again! Today's blog is about one of the best meals I've ever had with my family at home. It was lunch last Sunday. We don't often eat together at lunchtime at the weekends ^{1} _____. But last Sunday we were all at home because it was too snowy to go out. My brother and I decided to make a meal for everyone. We couldn't go out to buy anything ^{2} _____. There was a chicken, which we roasted, and onions, potatoes, carrots, tomatoes and beans, ^{3} _____. While it was cooking, my mum made a chocolate dessert. The food was amazing, but the reason I enjoyed it so much was the great feeling of being with all my family in our lovely warm home, ^{4} _____.

A and we eat the same kind of food
B so we used everything that we found in the fridge
C while it was snowing outside
D which we baked all together with a bit of oil and goat's cheese for about 40 minutes
E because we're usually out doing different activities

 PREPARE FOR THE EXAM

Listening Part 2

1 For each question, write the correct answer in the gap. Write **one word** or **a number** or **a date** or **a time**.

19

You will hear a boy telling his friend about another friend's birthday meal.

JASON'S BIRTHDAY MEAL

Name of restaurant: *Roberto's*
Day: (1) _____
Time: (2) _____ p.m.
Cost of meal: (3) £ _____ per person
Address of restaurant: (4) 74 _____ Street
Restaurant is opposite: (5) the _____

 EXAM TIPS

- Look at the notes before you listen and think about the information you'll need to write.
- Write numbers in figures (8) instead of words (eight). It's quicker and easier.

WRITING   An instant message

1 You and two friends, Nick and Joe, are going to make a cake for your teacher. Read the messages and complete them with the phrases in the box.

could one of you	how about
I'm not sure about	it's a good idea
why don't you	

Hi, we need to make the cake for Mr Yates. Are you free tomorrow evening? If you are, ¹ _____ making a chocolate cake? Everybody likes chocolate cake; it's quite easy and I've got a good recipe. ² _____ come to my place to make the cake? And ³ _____ get the ingredients tomorrow, please? I'm busy all day. I'll send you the recipe. Nick

Hi Nick, yes, I'm free tomorrow evening. ⁴ _____ making a chocolate cake. It's a bit boring. How about making a pineapple and coconut cake? I've got a great recipe. Sorry, but I haven't got time to get the ingredients tomorrow. ⁵ _____ to make the cake at your place. Your kitchen is nice and big. Joe

2 Write a message to Nick and answer his questions. Use the notes below.

- tomorrow evening – you're free
- chocolate cake – a good idea
- ingredients – yes, tomorrow morning
- make the cake at Nick's place? no – your place?

Hi Nick, yes, I'm free tomorrow evening.

_____
_____
_____
_____
_____
_____
_____

20 LIFE CHANGES

VOCABULARY *Change* as a verb and noun

1 Match the sentences.

1 I'm going to the department store to change some shoes. ......
2 I don't have to change trains. ......
3 I haven't had a change of address. ......
4 I'm taking a change of clothes. ......
5 I need to change this twenty-pound note. ......
6 I'm changing my life. ......
7 I think this will make a nice change. ......
8 Change will be difficult for me. ......

a I'll need something else to wear after working in Grandma's garden.
b I need to get fitter.
c I still live there.
d I'm going to have eggs for breakfast today instead of fruit.
e I want a drink from the drinks machine.
f I like things as they are now.
g I need a larger size.
h I stay on the same one all the way.

2 Complete the sentences with *a change* or *to change.*

1 I think Arlo wants .... his job.
2 Please let us know if you have .... of address.
3 Is it possible .... ten dollars?
4 I think .... will be good for you.
5 It was a long journey across the city. We had .... buses four times.
6 Make sure you bring .... of clothes for the trip. It's going to snow!
7 I'd like .... this video game, please.
8 It was sunny today. That was .... from all the rain we've had this week.

3 Read the sentences. Is *change* a noun or a verb in each one? Write *N* (noun) or *V* (verb).

0 Does Arlo want to change his job? ..*V*..
1 Please let us know your change of address. ......
2 Can you change a twenty-pound note? ......
3 It was a long journey. We had to change trains four times. ......
4 Bring a change of clothes for the trip. It's going to snow! ......

GRAMMAR Past simple passive

1 Tick (✓) the sentences which you think are the most probable.

1 a Jim ate some fish last night. ......
  b Jim was eaten by a fish last night. ......
2 a The baby was driven home from the hospital. ......
  b The baby drove home from the hospital. ......
3 a The dog gave its owner some meat. ......
  b The dog was given some meat by its owner. ......
4 a The teacher taught the lesson. ......
  b The teacher was taught the lesson. ......
5 a Nadya asked to clean her bedroom. ......
  b Nadya was asked to clean her bedroom. ......

2 Complete the sentences with the past simple passive form of the verbs in brackets.

1 The Statue of Liberty .... (give) to the USA by France.
2 A film .... (make) in our street. My brother and I were in it!
3 The cathedral and castle in our town .... (visit) by thousands of tourists last summer.
4 The new museum .... (complete) in 2012.
5 My room .... (decorate) last year.
6 We .... (take) around the cathedral by a guide.
7 Buckingham Palace .... (build) in the 18th century.

3 Rewrite the sentences in the passive. Use *by* when necessary.

0 Serena Williams won the singles gold medal at the Olympics.
The singles gold medal at the Olympics was won by Serena Williams.

1 Adam and Kevin Pearce set up the LoveYourBrain foundation in 2014.

2 The president opened the new museum last summer.

3 They opened the royal gardens to the public in 2002.

4 My parents gave me this leather bag when I went to high school.

5 Someone gave these expensive paintings to our local museum.

6 Last year, over three million people visited the Empire State Building.

4 Correct the mistakes in the sentences.

1 My old shorts was eaten by my dog.

2 I am selling my little home in the centre of town. It was build 25 years ago.

3 My birthday party was very enjoyable. All the people were danced.

4 My mobile is fantastic. It were made in Mexico.

5 Do you know about my new flat? I was moved there two weeks ago.

VOCABULARY — Life changes

1 Which event usually happens first in each pair? Tick (✓) the correct sentences.

0 You learn to talk.	You are born. ✓
1 You learn to talk.	You become a teenager.
2 You start working.	You go to high school.
3 You get married.	You start school.
4 You learn to walk.	You travel.
5 You take exams.	You are born.

2 Complete the text with the words in the box.

became	born	change	found	moved
take	training	travel	work	

My sister was [1] _____ in 1998, so she's a few years older than me. When we were young, we [2] _____ house many times, so she had to [3] _____ schools a lot, too. Since she left school, she has done a lot of jobs. First, she [4] _____ a taxi driver. She had to [5] _____ a difficult exam to do that job. But she found the long hours really hard so she looked for another job. She started [6] _____ as a receptionist in a hotel, but she didn't like the manager there, so she decided to [7] _____ to France where she [8] _____ part-time work in a restaurant in Lyon. She went to French classes when she wasn't at work. However, she started to miss home, so she came back and she's just started [9] _____ to be a police officer.

1 Read the biography and number the paragraphs in the correct order.

A Biography of my Father

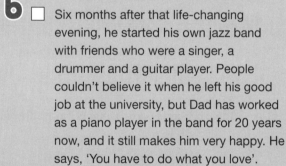

a ☐ After he left school, he went to Exeter University to study history. He did very well at university, and when his course finished, he moved to Durham and got a job at the university there. He taught history. He really enjoyed helping the students learn, and while he was doing this job, he became a writer. He wrote two books about the history of twentieth-century Europe. Unfortunately, he also stopped playing the piano.

b ☐ Six months after that life-changing evening, he started his own jazz band with friends who were a singer, a drummer and a guitar player. People couldn't believe it when he left his good job at the university, but Dad has worked as a piano player in the band for 20 years now, and it still makes him very happy. He says, 'You have to do what you love'.

c ☐ My father was born in Edinburgh, Scotland, on 5th January 1970. When he was a boy, his grandmother gave Dad her beautiful old piano. He quickly learned to play it, and he practised every day. He soon became very good at it. When he grew up, he took this piano with him every time he moved house.

d ☐ One evening, before I was born, he went with my mother to a piano concert. This concert changed his life. While he was watching the woman playing the piano, he remembered how much he loved playing it. That night he sat down at the piano that he was given as a child and began playing again.

2 Read *A Biography of my Father* again and number the changes in his life in the order they happened.

a He went to live and work in Durham. ....
b He changed his job. ....
c He started to play the piano very well. ....
d He started writing books. ....
e He was born. _1_
f He studied at Exeter University. ....
g He went to a concert which changed his life. ....
h He was given a piano. ....

PREPARE FOR THE EXAM

Listing Part 3

1 For each question, choose the correct answer.

 You will hear Robert talking to his friend Penny about moving house.

1 When is Robert moving?
  A in May   **B** in June   **C** in July

2 Robert is moving to
  A Leeds.   **B** Liverpool.   **C** York.

3 Penny will visit Robert by
  A train.   **B** bus.   **C** car.

4 Why is Robert moving?
  A His dad wants a new job.   **B** His mum is changing jobs.   **C** His mum is becoming a student.

5 How does Robert feel about moving?
  A worried   **B** sad   **C** excited

EXAM TIPS

- You hear each recording in the listening exam twice. Use the second time to check your answers.
- You will hear all three answers in the conversation – listen carefully for the correct one.

WRITING   A biography

1 Read *A Biography of my Father* on page 82 again and match the paragraphs (a–d) to the headings.

1 An important event that changes my father's life   ....

2 My father leaves home, finishes his studies and starts work   ....

3 My father's life today   ....

4 My father's early life   ....

2 Write a short biography of an adult you know. Use *A Biography of my Father* on page 82 to help you. Write four short paragraphs using the structure and ideas below.

1 The person's early life
For example: where and when they were born, what they liked doing as a child.

2 What the person did when she / he left home
For example: what job / training they did, where they studied, where they lived.

3 An important event that changed this person's life
For example: they got married, they changed jobs, they moved city.

4 This person's life now
For example: what they do now, where they live, if they are happy.

Acknowledgements

The authors and publishers acknowledge the following sources of copyright material and are grateful for the permissions granted. While every effort has been made, it has not always been possible to identify the sources of all the material used, or to trace all copyright holders. If any omissions are brought to our notice, we will be happy to include the appropriate acknowledgements on reprinting and in the next update to the digital edition, as applicable.

Key: U = Unit.

Text
U3: Brooklyn Free School for the text about Brooklyn Free School. Copyright © Brooklyn Free School. Reproduced with kind permission.

Photography
The following images are sourced from Getty Images.

U1: Tony Anderson/The Image Bank; a_Taiga/iStock/Getty Images Plus; U2: Alan Novelli/DigitalVision; Gianni Sarasso/Moment; Frank and Helena/Cultura; David Cayless/Photodisc; Arnaud Bertrande/Moment; U3: yotrak/iStock/Getty Images Plus; Corbis/VCG/Corbis; Zachery T Jensen (ztj@me.com)/Momen; VvoeVale/iStock/Getty Images Plus; heinstirred/Stock Editorial/Getty Images Plus; Victor Fraile/Corbis; U4: pamspix/iStock/Getty Images Plus; Mint Images - Tim Robbins; Photography taken by Mario Gutiérrez/Moment; Alberto Manuel Urosa Toledano/Moment Unreleased; Rocter/iStock/Getty Images Plus; U5: Geri Lavrov/Photographer's Choice; Purestock; Kerkez/iStock/Getty Images Plus; monkeybusinessimages/iStock/Getty Images Plus; Keith Brofsky/UpperCut Images; Martin Harvey/Photolibrary; U6: Taek-sang Jeong/iStock/Getty Images Plus; s-cphoto/E+; Grassetto/iStock/Getty Images Plus; Orhan Senol/EyeEm; DEVASHISH_RAWAT/iStock/Getty Images Plus; caracterdesign/E+; Topic Images Inc.; Maskot; pbombaert/Moment; pbombaert/Moment; Martin Siepmann/imageBROKER; U7: Hero Images; akrp/E+; JohnGollop/iStock Unreleased; U8: Jacek Kadaj/Moment; Trio Images/Photodisc; David Leahy/DigitalVision; Paper Boat Creative/The Image Bank; U9: PT Images/Tetra images; Ken Fisher/The Image Bank; Jenny Elia Pfeiffer/Corbis; Robin Skjoldborg/Taxi; iPandastudio/iStock/Getty Images Plus; grandriver/E+; RedChopsticks/redchopsticks; Jon Hicks/Photographer's Choice; gorodenkoff/iStock/Getty Images Plus; IMAGEMORE Co, Ltd.; U10: Maskot; Ken Welsh/Alamy Stock Photo; Highwaystarz-Photography/iStock/Getty Images Plus; IvonneW/iStock/Getty Images Plus; U11: kokka/iStock Unreleased; Christian Kober/AWL Images; LightFieldStudios/iStock/Getty Images Plus; U12: Dimitrios Kambouris/Getty Images Entertainment; Hero Images; Westend61; U13: anatoliy_gleb/iStock/Getty Images Plus; Juice Images; Hero Images; U14: Viktor Holm/Folio; Adha Ghazali/EyeEm; U15: Marc Romanelli/Blend Images; Hero Images; Jose Luis Pelaez Inc./Blend Images; Compassionate Eye Foundation/Gabriela; Medina/DigitalVision; Image Source; Rafa Fernndez/EyeEm; Jonatan Fernstrom/Stockbyte; Westend61; hudiemm/E+; benimage/E+; bravo1954/E+; Pamee/EyeEm; Teh/EyeEm; Emmanuelle Bonzami/EyeEm; Eugen Wais/EyeEm; TenevArt/iStock/Getty Images Plus; nikolay100; imo-piano/iStock/Getty Images Plus; U17: SergeyIT/iStock/Getty Images Plus; Dennie Cody and Duangkamon Khattiya/Photodisc; skynesher/E+; SolStock/E+; Dave Fimbres Photography/Moment Open; Granger Wootz/Blend Images; Tom Grill/Photographer's Choice RF; U18: Radius Images; Don Mason/Blend Images; Burak Karademir/Moment; amazingmikael/iStock/Getty Images Plus; Stígur Már Karlsson /Heimsmyndir/E+; U19: Zoonar RF; JGI/Jamie Grill/Blend Images; Hinterhaus Productions/Taxi; William Reavell/Dorling Kindersley; Guerilla; U20: Gary Cralle/The Image Bank; fatihhoca/iStock/Getty Images Plus; Hybrid Images/Cultura.

The following photographs have been sourced from other library/sources.

U3: GeoPic/Alamy Stock Photo; U10: Ken Welsh/Alamy Stock Photo; U12: Courtesy of Brooklyn Free School.

Front cover photography by fanjianhua/ Moment/Getty Images.

Illustration
Mark Draisey; Russ Cook; Dusan Lakicevic (Beehive Illustration); Nigel Dobbyn (Beehive Illustration).

The publishers are grateful to the following contributors: author of Cambridge English Prepare! First Edition Level 3 Workbook: Garan Holcombe; cover design and design concept: restless; typesetting: emc design Ltd; audio recordings: produced by Leon Chambers and recorded at The SoundHouse Studios, London; project management: Louise Davoren